Untying the Knot:
Your Guide to a Successful New Jersey Divorce

Karen N. Grayson-Rodgers, Esq.,
Rhonda L. Rivera, Esq.,
Cindy D. Salvo, Esq.

Aventine Press

Published by Aventine Press
750 State St. #319
San Diego CA, 92101
www.aventinepress.com

ISBN: 1-59330-702-0

Printed in the United States of America

TABLE OF CONTENTS

CHAPTER THREE

14 Important Dos and Don'ts for a
Successful New Jersey Divorce

Illustrations in Chapter Two by Candace Rowden Bassat. Candace is a retired Special Education school teacher who always had a secret desire to be a cartoonist.

WHY WE WROTE THIS BOOK

If you are one of the many people in New Jersey who are currently facing the prospect of divorce, we wrote this book for you. This is undoubtedly a difficult time for you emotionally. The last thing you need is to allow your emotions to guide you blindly down this road, without being armed with the important information you need to know to properly face the journey that lies ahead.

Divorce has sometimes been compared to death. It certainly is a life-changing experience, and change is frightening. Your "happily ever after" has been sabotaged, but now is the time to put your uncertain, angry, sad and disoriented feelings aside and tackle your divorce with a practical eye towards the future.

The goal of this book is to give you the power of information. We will debunk myths, answer the most frequently asked questions we get about divorce and let you know what you must DO and must NOT DO to have a successful New Jersey divorce.

Some people may wonder how we can use the word "successful" in the context of divorce. But, once divorce is inevitable, it is a "successful" divorce if it provides you with the best possible results with the least possible stress. That is what we try to achieve for all of our clients.

Hopefully you are reading this book at a preliminary stage — before you have taken any concrete steps towards divorce. That is, hopefully you have not yet told your spouse you are filing for divorce, have not moved out of your home, and so on. If that is the case, we can definitely help you avoid some of the pitfalls that may be ahead. If you have already taken steps towards divorce, hopefully they were not harmful ones, and we can help you get back on, or stay on, the right path.

We offer each of you — our readers — a complimentary initial consultation to discuss your divorce and see if we are a good fit to work together. If you decide not to hire us, or if we decline your case, we will provide you with a list of other experienced divorce attorneys in your area to help you continue your search for the right divorce attorney for you!

We wish you a successful New Jersey divorce.

Sincerely,
Karen Grayson-Rodgers, Esq., Rhonda L. Rivera, Esq. and Cindy D. Salvo, Esq.

Visit our website to learn more about The Salvo Law Firm's divorce practice: www.salvolawfirm.com or call us at 973-233-4080.

CHAPTER ONE
7 Myths about Divorce

We will start out this book by telling you the seven most common myths about divorce. You may hear — or will hear — these myths many times, especially once you tell your family and friends that you are seeking a divorce. The person who tells you any of these seven myths means well. Perhaps the person heard it on a television show, or read it in a magazine article, or is passing it along from a friend. In any event, when someone offers you any of these seven myths, smile politely and say thank you. Then, immediately discard the "advice" and continue with the plan you and your divorce attorney have established. Everyone means well, but no one is privy to all of the information you share with your divorce attorney. Remember, every divorce is different, just as every marriage is different. You are in a unique situation. Trust in your divorce attorney's expertise to help you successfully navigate the process!

So, here are the seven myths about divorce — what makes them myths, the truth behind them and how *not* to get caught up in them:

1. *"What's Mine Is Yours, and What's Yours Is Mine"*

Back at the beginning of your marriage, if someone were to ask you if this saying were true, you probably would have said yes. Whatever your spouse bought or even brought into the marriage was equally available to both of you, without question.

That was then. Your circumstances, unfortunately, have changed. Remember the scene in the movie *When Harry Met Sally*, where Harry (a divorcé) tells his newly engaged friends Jess and Marie to put their names in each of their books to show to whom it belongs, so as to avoid fighting over them later in divorce court? This is now your new reality.

In the state of New Jersey, only assets acquired <u>during</u> the marriage are subject to the "what's mine is yours, and what's yours is mine" school of thought, otherwise known as "equitable distribution." Gifts and inheritances are considered separate property, as are the assets you each brought into the marriage (like Jess's and Marie's books), unless these assets were commingled during your married years together.

What does this all mean? What if, for example, before you were married, a relative died and left you $20,000, and you then took that money and put it into a CD in your name? If you kept letting the CD roll over and reinvested the interest with the principal since Day 1, then this $20,000 plus interest would not be considered marital property subject to equitable distribution. It is truly separate property and will be excluded from the divorce asset distribution. So, in this particular case, "What's mine is mine!"

However, what if you took the same premarital $20,000 inheritance, and instead of investing it in a CD, you put it into your personal money market account. After you and your spouse were married, you used that $20,000 as a down payment on a jointly owned house. Now, even though the funds were in an account under your name only, you commingled the funds with your spouse's to purchase the marital residence. You cannot now reclaim sole right to the $20,000 in a divorce settlement. In other words, in this situation, "What's mine is yours."

This brings up another situation: when title is in one spouse's name for an asset purchased during the marriage. If your spouse bought a car during your marriage but the title is in just your spouse's name, is that car subject to equitable distribution? The answer is yes, usually. Marriage is a joint entity, so to speak, and any acquisitions made during the marriage — regardless of who holds legal title — are jointly owned. When the joint entity (your marriage) is dissolved, the assets are then divided unless, of course, proof exists that such asset was a gift or was purchased with separate money. This general proposition of equitable distribution applies to all assets including businesses, real estate, cars, paintings, and so forth. "What's yours is mine."

As you can probably tell from this short discussion, dividing up assets is extremely fact-based and requires an experienced divorce attorney who understands all of the intricacies of your particular situation. Knowing the truth is the only way your attorney can advocate effectively for you to have a fair distribution of assets. While "What's mine is yours, and what's yours is mine" is a cute saying, it does not always carry legal significance. Only an experienced divorce attorney will be able to help you navigate this aspect of the process to a successful conclusion.

2. *"My Spouse Was a Shop-a-holic, so I'm Divorcing the Debt Too!"*

If only this myth were true! If your spouse was a shop-a-holic during your marriage, accumulating debt at every possible turn, generally you will not be able to avoid paying back those debts through your divorce. This is true even if the credit cards were solely in your spouse's name.

As we have just mentioned, in New Jersey, marriage is considered to be a type of joint entity. What one or the other spouse buys, spends or acquires during the marriage goes into this joint entity. For example, if one spouse buys a sailboat, and solely takes out a loan to do so, both parties to the marriage (plus any children) will be able to enjoy the sailboat. Upon divorcing, the other spouse cannot avoid the liability for the sailboat by claiming she never learned how to sail and never operated it alone. The sailboat loan is a shared obligation that will be taken into account in a divorce settlement.

Even if one spouse racked up a huge debt at a specialty clothing store catering to one sex, and the other spouse could not possibly wear the clothes purchased in that store, the debt is still a shared obligation incurred during the marriage. This debt will be considered a liability of both parties and cannot be avoided by the nonwearer spouse via divorce.

If you can step back from your situation and look at this proposition objectively, you will see why this rule makes sense. When credit was extended to both of you, or just one party to the marriage, usually a credit report was run. While each individual has his or her own credit score, the two of you contributed to each other's score during your marriage. Certain financial decisions made by both of you reflect upon both of your credit scores, such as jointly buying a house, taking out a home equity line of credit, paying household and other bills timely, and so forth. So, even when only one spouse acquires a debt, the reality is that you both were somehow involved in its approval.

That said, there are times when one spouse's debt is not considered a joint debt in New Jersey divorce proceedings. In order to avoid the presumption of a shared obligation, you will have to prove your soon-to-be former spouse accumulated the debt by "nefarious behavior" — underhanded, sneaky or simply bad acts. Did your spouse amass this debt as a result of an affair, by buying expensive presents, hotel rooms or trips, without your knowledge? Is your spouse addicted to drugs or alcohol and accrued this debt to perpetuate his or her habit, unbeknownst to you? These are facts that a New Jersey court will take into account when deciding whether a liability is a shared obligation for purposes of a divorce settlement.

Once again, an experienced New Jersey divorce attorney must guide you through this financial maze. Honesty with your attorney is key to coming up with a fair and equitable plan for your divorce. Whether you are the spouse that accumulated the debt or you are on the receiving end of this situation, make your divorce attorney aware of the circumstances. The path to a successful divorce hinges on your attorney being presented with all of the facts before the proceedings even begin.

3. *"My Sister/Brother/Boss/Friend Went through a Divorce, and Told Me..."*

Let's face it — almost everyone knows someone who has gone through, or is going through, a divorce. (Indeed, statistics show that approximately 40–50 percent of Americans are divorcing or have been divorced). So, you are certainly not alone.

When people learn you are about to go through a divorce, they will often reach out to you and offer advice — whether solicited or not — to "help" you. They mean well, and often just want to stop your pain, ease your fears or simply make you look ahead to better times. There is nothing wrong with being a good friend and offering support to help someone through a bad situation.

Given that you have already decided to end your marriage, or your spouse has decided this for you, you should take advantage of all the well-wishes and diversions your family and friends have to offer. Cry on their shoulders, go to the movies with them, enjoy a camping trip with them, eat out, go to the beach, take in a Broadway play with them. Remember that you deserve to be happy and to have stretches of time where you don't even think about your upcoming divorce. Your family and friends are very important to your future, so let them take care of you a little bit now.

Friends and family will emotionally support you through your divorce. However, they will not be the ones guiding you through the legal process required to secure your divorce. With that in mind, *please* do not take any advice they give you about the process. While they are undoubtedly very well-intentioned, they simply cannot give you accurate counsel for your divorce.

As you can glean from this discussion, every divorce turns on its specific facts. What may be the best resolution in one divorce is not necessarily the right outcome for your situation. Only your divorce attorney will be able to analyze all of your facts and apply them to the law so that the best result, for your circumstances, can be achieved.

4. *"The Mother Always Gets the House and Custody of the Kids"*

Years ago, in cases of divorce, the court usually ordered that the mother would stay in the marital home and have primary custody of the children. The father would have visitation rights perhaps every other weekend. This may have been the situation you grew up in or knew about from your school friends.

Just as with everything from the advent of personal computers and the Internet, to styles of dress, music and the evening news, divorce laws and norms have evolved over the years. This is true in New Jersey, as well as everywhere else in the country. What was a "routine arrangement" for divorce in the 1900s can be nearly unrecognizable in the 2000s.

So, what is the "usual" arrangement nowadays for housing and custody in a New Jersey divorce? With the caveat that there is nothing "usual" about divorce, the following are the options courts typically consider when dealing with these issues:

With respect to deciding who gets the marital home, the question is definitely not "who wants to stay in the house more." Rather, a New Jersey court will probably consider the circumstances such as the size of the house and suitability for the children's needs in determining whether the custodial parent should remain in the house.

If you believe you will have primary custody (much more about that topic later), you should take many factors into account before arguing to stay in the house. While you may have taken many years to decorate the house to your liking, and spent much time and effort trying to make it a comfortable home for your family, a house is — first and foremost — a very big undertaking. You must consider whether you have the financial ability not only to pay the mortgage, taxes, utilities and insurance, but also lawn maintenance, snow removal and for the unexpected repairs that come with home ownership. If your spouse routinely fixed things in the house, now you may have to pay a maintenance person for these repairs. Child support and spousal support (alimony) will only take you so far, so make sure your income is sufficient to cover these liabilities. Remember, a house is a building, but a home is made wherever your family lives.

Children and "who gets them" are the issue of paramount importance in many divorces. The two words, "custody battle," strike fear in many people's hearts and sometimes prevent them from seeking a divorce, even if they are unhappy in the marriage. So, how does the custody decision work in New Jersey?

In New Jersey, the "best interests of the child(ren)" is the factor that is most analyzed in order to determine the custody arrangement following divorce. A New Jersey court will look at the following factors, among others, in making a custody determination: (1) the emotional and physical environment with each parent; (2) the personal safety of the child; (3) the mental and physical health of the parents; (4) the age of the child; (5) the preference of the child (if the child is old enough — courts typically start paying attention to the child's preference once he/

she reaches the age of 12 or 13); (6) the prior behavior of the parents, including any history of abuse; (7) the ability of each parent to care for the child; and (8) the importance of religious upbringing within the family. Barring abuse or addiction, it is presumed to be in their best interests that the children spend as much time as possible with both parents.

In New Jersey, custody is divided into two parts: legal and physical. With legal custody, the spouse has the ability to make the major decisions about the child's health, education, safety and welfare. Physical custody simply refers to with whom the child resides. A custody arrangement, therefore, can take the form of (1) sole physical or legal custody; (2) sole physical custody with joint legal custody; or (3) joint custody. Be aware that the term "joint" does not mean "equal" but rather that both spouses equally share the obligation to raise the child. It is by far the most common arrangement to have shared joint legal custody, with one spouse receiving sole physical custody. Then, the noncustodial parent will be granted visitation rights, provided there is no compelling reason why he/she shouldn't be given visitation with the children.

As will be echoed throughout this book, you must disclose all the facts and details to your divorce attorney when trying to determine whether to keep the house or what type of custody arrangements are best for your particular situation. Your lawyer will outline all of the possibilities and together you will decide what the best result is. These decisions are neither easy nor routine, and your attorney will help guide you through the process. Together, you are creating the building blocks for your successful New Jersey divorce and, ultimately, your future.

5. *"Your Divorce Will Be Decided during a Trial, by a Judge."*

The traditional concept of how a divorce is obtained is embodied in the 1979 film *Kramer vs. Kramer*. In the movie, both spouses made their pleas for custody in the courtroom, and ultimately no one was happy with the outcome ordered by the judge. During the trial, both spouses suffered character assassinations on the stand and were forced publicly to admit damaging facts about themselves.

Fast-forward to the reality of today's divorce protocols. In New Jersey, fewer than 10 percent of couples go to trial to end their marriages. The courts have recognized that, in most cases, the parties to the divorce are the best arbiters of how it should be dissolved. Moreover, the sheer number of cases filed in New Jersey courts do not allow for a speedy determination of all the issues. As a result, now most divorces are settled either in mediation or arbitration settings, with the end result either being a Marital Settlement Agreement negotiated by the parties with the help of their lawyers and/or mediator or a decision rendered by the arbitrator.

In mediation, the two spouses and their attorneys meet with the mediator in an informal setting and come to a decision about all of their issues. The mediator's role is to facilitate negotiation. The mediator does not make the decisions for the parties; rather, the husband and the wife, with the help of their attorneys, determine the best outcome for their situation. At the conclusion of the mediation, which may take days, weeks or months, the mediator drafts a Memorandum of Understanding, which will be incorporated, once finalized, into a formal Interspousal Agreement signed by both parties.

By contrast, arbitration is more formal and the arbitrator decides the issues. While not conducted in a courtroom, arbitration does involve documents and testimony elicited by attorneys. The key differences between an arbitration hearing and a court proceeding are that the arbitrator is selected by the parties rather than assigned by the court system, the rules that govern litigation are relaxed and the arbitrator will make a decision promptly after the evidence is presented. Once that decision is presented to the judge, your divorce is final.

Mediation or arbitration can be entered into voluntarily by the couple either before the complaint for divorce is ever filed, or after it is filed and litigation about the divorce has begun. In addition, a judge will send a case to mandatory mediation if custody and/or parenting time is at issue. Mandatory financial mediation is required if the parties cannot settle their monetary issues at an early settlement panel before the trial date. In all cases, New Jersey law provides a mechanism of last resort for the judge to decide any disputes that are not resolved by settlement.

The fact that litigated divorces can take years to become final and can eat away at your life savings in legal fees supports a decision to choose mediation or arbitration. Any good will that still exists between you and your spouse may be eroded through a lengthy litigation. For your sake, and that of your children, you may want to consider mediation as a path to a successful divorce.

An answer to normal concerns of "Will mediation allow one spouse to steamroll the other?" or "Will the more affluent spouse, or the more educated spouse, or simply the more boisterous spouse have an edge if no judge is present?" is a simple No! If the mediator (or arbitrator) senses an imbalance of power between the husband and wife, the mediator (or arbitrator) is required to send the case back to the courtroom for a judge to oversee. Furthermore, mediation is as nonadversarial as the legal system can make it, allowing you and your soon-to-be former spouse to identify your particular issues and figure out workable solutions. By starting with mediation, you are not giving up your right to litigate your divorce; you are just giving yourself a workable framework in which to start the next chapter of your life.

When you consult with your divorce attorney prior to filing the complaint, he or she will go over the various options with you — mediation, arbitration and litigation. Only after carefully reviewing the pros and cons of each process in the context of your particular circumstances will you both be able to decide which option is best for you. Sometimes the best option may be to just have a settlement conference with your attorneys to arrive at a settlement, allowing for a quick resolution without the added cost of mediation, arbitration or litigation.

Once an agreement is reached, the judge will not approve nor disapprove the settlement. You will attend a brief hearing where either your lawyer or the judge will ask you and your soon-to-be ex-spouse a series of questions to ensure that the agreement was entered into voluntarily, that you believe the agreement to be fair and reasonable given the circumstances, that you understand it and are not under the influence of drugs or alcohol which would impair your ability to understand the agreement, and that there was no undue influence or duress. If the judge is comfortable in accepting that both parties are comfortable with the settlement, the divorce will be entered without the judge even reading the settlement agreement. Therefore, it is very important that you listen to your lawyer to be sure you understand what is happening at each stage of the divorce process. Having a lawyer who understands what you want and will advocate in your best interest is essential to a positive outcome, but you must fully understand what it is you are agreeing to! Make sure your lawyer keeps you involved from beginning to end so the final result is understood and accepted by you.

6. *"The Court Will Side with Me Because My Spouse Caused Our Divorce"*

Emotions play a huge role in your path to divorce — how could they not? Your "I do" has become "I don't." Whatever led up to your decision to end your marriage, you are now faced with "untying the knot," both legally and emotionally.

As you know, the court is charged with overseeing your divorce proceedings to ensure that all the legalities in dividing up your assets, caring for your children and addressing financial responsibilities are resolved. In doing so, the court looks to the best interests of your children and equitable distribution of assets. As much as possible, the court attempts to view a divorce as an unwinding of a type of business venture, and to be as fair as possible to both parties.

Towards that end, New Jersey has adopted a "no fault" divorce. What that means is that the person who files the divorce complaint (the "petitioner") only has to allege that, for a period of at least six months, "irreconcilable differences" arose that led to a breakdown of the marriage for which there is no "reasonable prospect of reconciliation." Who "caused" the divorce does not have to be disclosed. And even if it is disclosed, it is irrelevant in the eyes of the law in order to obtain a divorce, even if, for example, one spouse has been cheating and the other has not.

The "no fault" divorce is a relatively recent change to the divorce laws in New Jersey. Prior to January 20, 2007, in order to get a divorce, a petitioner had to allege adultery, mental illness, addiction or extreme cruelty, among other possible grounds. So, just a few years ago, the fact that your spouse "caused" your divorce was relevant to your divorce proceeding. Times have changed and, as we have just stated, New Jersey no longer requires a petitioner to state the reason for a divorce (although you can still sue using adultery, cruelty, and so on. as grounds, if you want to).

If your spouse cheated on you with the gardener, lost all of your savings in a poker game, or became an alcoholic, you are understandably emotional and want to tell everyone who will listen how you were wronged. You may have feelings of insecurity, anger, guilt and anxiety that you want to share. This is only natural. A time and place exists for such disclosures — tell your therapist, friends, family members, online community and/or religious counselor. These people either are trained to help you or will give you much needed support with your decision to divorce.

The Courts of the State of New Jersey generally are no longer the proper forum to air such details, however. The judge, mediator or arbitrator is trained in the law, a decidedly nonemotional-based system. His or her job is to apply the law to your facts and circumstances in order to "unwind" your "joint venture."

Note, however, that in dealing with child custody issues, it is often appropriate — and important — to let the court know that your spouse cheated, abused drugs, and the like. Once again, the only proper person who can advise you about what to divulge to the court — and when — is your divorce attorney. Your lawyer will guide you on these issues in order to arrive at the best end to your marriage.

7. *"All Divorce Attorneys Are Alike"*

Throughout this book so far, references have been made to one of the most important people who will be coming into your life: your divorce attorney. Your lawyer will help you navigate the legal process and be instrumental in your having a successful divorce.

If you broke your ankle, would you go to an Ear, Nose & Throat doctor? Of course not! Similarly, when choosing your divorce attorney, you don't want to go to a "corporate-lawyer-who-is-friends-with-your-best-friend's-father." Because this is a highly specialized field, you need to look for an attorney who regularly practices divorce law. A corporate lawyer may have the skills to negotiate a million-dollar deal but be utterly ineffectual in negotiating a spousal support agreement because he has no understanding of the divorce laws and what your rights are.

Now, how do you sort through all of the attorneys who specialize in divorce law in New Jersey to find the right one for you? Do you check out the Yellow Pages, do a Google search, respond to newspaper/radio/TV ads, or ask friends for referrals? These sources could be a good starting point to help you develop a list of attorneys from which to select.

Just as one doctor does not suit every patient, not every divorce attorney is a good match for everyone. When you meet with an attorney to see if you are going to hire him or her, you should keep the following factors in mind:

- First, you need to look for an experienced divorce attorney. The lawyer should be well-versed in the complex legal issues that inevitably will arise during the divorce process. An attorney who has been practicing in the field for many years will have acquired both the legal and practical knowledge necessary to effectively and expediently secure your divorce.

- Second, you need to ascertain the divorce attorney's goals. You want someone who will fiercely fight for you and your best interests. Your divorce attorney needs to be willing to fight for the best possible result for you and to protect your children from the process as much as possible.

- Third, you need to be comfortable with the lawyer's demeanor. Make sure the attorney does not talk in "legalese" but rather explains the divorce process to you using plain English. If you don't understand something, ask for clarification. If the attorney seems annoyed at having to explain something to you again, you should probably look for another attorney! The attorney also should be willing to respond to your telephone calls within 24 hours (or less!) and should be willing to keep you informed of all aspects of your divorce case. Remember, you are going to be revealing highly personal information about yourself, your marriage and your finances to this person, so you must establish a comfortable and trusting relationship.

- Fourth, when interviewing a potential divorce attorney, keep your ultimate goal of a successful divorce in mind. If you want an amicable and swift resolution, you want an attorney who is willing to help you do this. He or she should be able to be diplomatic with the other side — you don't want an attorney who wants to turn every molehill into a mountain and run up huge legal bills! On the other hand, if you want your attorney to be aggressive, and fight for you as vigorously as the law will allow, you must hire an attorney who is willing to do so. You must discuss the approach you want your attorney to take during the initial consultation, and make sure he or she is onboard with your decision.

- Fifth, your attorney should be empathetic and supportive of you during the divorce process — especially if you are very emotional about what you are going through. Some divorce attorneys are "all business" and are unwilling or unable to provide you with the emotional support you might need during this difficult time of your life. Did you know that the most common complaint people have about their divorce attorneys is that they don't return their telephone calls? That behavior is really inexcusable. You must make sure the divorce attorney you choose is committed to providing you with legal expertise and emotional support.

17

- Sixth, you need to inquire as to the divorce attorney's fee to ensure that it is affordable to you. Most lawyers will require a payment of several thousand dollars up front, called a retainer, and then will bill you using an hourly rate. As an attorney works on your case, he/she will deduct the time spent from the retainer until it is depleted, and then will require you to replenish the retainer until your case is finished. If there is any money remaining on your retainer at the end of the representation, the attorney will return it to you.

As you can see, many factors go into your decision as to who will represent you in your divorce. While it may be convenient for late-night talk-show hosts to lump all lawyers together as a single group, not all attorneys are alike by any means. Only after you meet with and learn your attorney's experience, style, demeanor, goals and fees will you be comfortable with your selection and know he or she is the right one for you. Together, you will navigate the road to a successful divorce.

CHAPTER TWO

Answers to the 21 Most Frequently Asked Questions about Divorce

At this point in your decision-making process, you have determined that you want to leave your spouse and start a new life on your own. Or your spouse has made that decision for you. But, you probably have so many questions about the *unknown*: finances, children/pets and the legal process of getting a divorce in New Jersey. This section of the book will answer the 7 Most Frequently Asked Questions in each of these three categories:

1. **About finances**

Couples fight about money more than any other issue, and disputes over money cause the breakup of more marriages than any other reason. In the divorce law arena, how are financial issues resolved? Here are the 7 Most Frequently Asked Questions most clients ask — or think about but are too embarrassed to ask — about finances.

a. My spouse cheated — how can I take him/her to the cleaners?

As discussed in Myth #6 in the previous chapter, the cause of your divorce is no longer relevant to the New Jersey courts.

New Jersey has enacted "no fault" divorce grounds, meaning that if your spouse cheated, it is not necessary to let the court know about it in order for a divorce to be granted. In other words, you can obtain a divorce just by telling the court that you have been living separate and apart for at least six months and don't have any reasonable hope for reconciliation.

One important note: Fault may be relevant in divorce proceedings, however, if children are involved and there is a custody dispute. Under those circumstances, filing for divorce based upon adultery — or abuse, addiction or criminal acts — may strategically assist you in getting a favorable child custody arrangement. In addition, fault may be relevant if it negatively affects the economic status of the parties; or if it so violates societal norms that continuing the economic bonds between the parties would confound notions of simple justice. These last two possibilities are very narrowly construed by the courts. This is a discussion you need to have with your attorney when strategizing about your divorce, as only your divorce attorney will know all of the facts and circumstances about your unique case.

So, how do you take your spouse "to the cleaners" in a divorce setting? Let's start with what this phrase means. "Taking someone to the cleaners" means that you take a significant portion of their money. Essentially what you are saying is that you want to punish your spouse by taking away something of extreme value (money) because that person was involved in taking something away from you that once meant a lot to you (your marriage). But New Jersey law provides a framework for dividing assets between you and your spouse upon divorce (called "equitable distribution"), and so taking your soon-to-be ex-spouse "to the cleaners" may not be possible. Of course, you can and should fight for whatever you legitimately have coming to you!

As will be discussed in greater detail later in this book, the purpose of equitable distribution of marital assets is to achieve a fair allocation between the two spouses of what was acquired during the marriage. Decisions about child and spousal support are based on a going-forward basis and take into account how much money is necessary to support the nonpayor spouse and to take care of the children. The final type and amount of equitable distribution, child support and alimony (a.k.a. spousal support) can be determined either by agreement of the parties or by decision of the judge. Your divorce attorney will fight for your "fair share" of the marital assets.

With that as a backdrop, there are ways to make your spouse "pay" for cheating on you, or destroying your marriage, but you must consider the consequences. You can extend the length of the divorce proceedings by being obstinate and increasing legal fees. Revenge is sweet, right? While this tactic sounds satisfying, think about what it would do to you: Not only will the legal battle be extended for your former spouse, it will be extended for you and your children as well, meaning your attorney's fees will be increased too. The longer the proceedings take, the more time you will have to spend dwelling on the past rather than creating a new future.

To sum up, in legal terms, a divorce essentially dissolves a business entity — your marriage. The law seeks to distribute marital assets, and award support, using a dispassionate approach. Trying to interject emotional needs such as guilt, revenge and punishment into the legal process, generally, is not necessary nor welcomed although totally understandable. Your divorce attorney (and therapist, if you decide to see one) will help you navigate these extremely difficult waters so that you achieve a successful divorce for your particular circumstances.

CRB

b. Does the wife get alimony for life?

Let's start this section by reviewing the question in detail: Asking if "the wife" receives alimony (now more often called "spousal support") is actually very misleading. In today's world, the husband may receive alimony as often as being required to pay it! Courts do not look at gender when deciding to whom to award alimony, but rather they determine which of the two spouses was the major breadwinner and may then award alimony to the more economically dependent spouse.

The last part of the question — whether alimony continues "for life" — has such a final sound to it, does it not? After all, prisoners are sent to jail "for life" after committing terrible crimes against humanity. The truth is, with respect to spousal support, the length of time it is required to be paid depends upon many different factors, and New Jersey courts favor a limited duration award.

With all of this in mind, the better question to ask is *"How long will spousal support need to be paid, if at all, and by whom?"* To get an answer, the New Jersey legislature has enacted a law, N.J.S.A. §2A:34-23(b), that identifies 13 factors that are considered by the courts in setting spousal support:

(1) The actual need and ability of the parties to pay;
(2) The duration of the marriage or civil union;

22

(3) The age, physical and emotional health of the parties;

(4) The standard of living established in the marriage or civil union and the likelihood that each party can maintain a reasonably comparable standard of living;

(5) The earning capacities, educational levels, vocational skills, and employability of the parties;

(6) The length of absence from the job market of the party seeking spousal support;

(7) The parental responsibilities for the children;

(8) The time and expense necessary to acquire sufficient education or training to enable the party seeking spousal support to find appropriate employment, the availability of the training and employment, and the opportunity for future acquisitions of capital assets and income;

(9) The history of the financial or nonfinancial contributions to the marriage or civil union by each party, including contributions to the care and education of the children and interruption of personal careers or educational opportunities;

(10) The equitable distribution of property ordered and any payouts on equitable distribution, directly or indirectly, out of current income, to the extent this consideration is reasonable, just and fair;

(11) The income available to either party through investment of any assets held by that party;

(12) The tax treatment and consequences to both parties of any award of spousal support, including the designation of all or a portion of the payment as a nontaxable payment; and

(13) Any other factors that the court may deem relevant.

There are five different types of spousal support that may be awarded in New Jersey: *pendente lite*, reimbursement, limited duration, rehabilitative and permanent. These different forms of spousal support may be awarded separately or in combination, if appropriate.

- *Alimony pendente lite* is the only form of spousal support temporarily awarded during the litigation of the divorce. This type of support allows the two parties to maintain the "status quo" until a full analysis of their financial affairs is achieved and usually expires when a final decree of divorce is entered.
- *Reimbursement alimony* recognizes the sacrifices one spouse made during the marriage, such as maintaining the house and/or working and turning over the money toward the other spouse's education or career development, in order to enhance that spouse's potential earning capacity and increase the couple's standard of living. This type of alimony usually is limited to the time it takes to repay the financial benefits that were provided by the supported spouse. Reimbursement alimony is designed to make a sacrificing spouse whole.
- *Limited duration alimony*, also known as "term alimony," is awarded when the marriage was short, but an economic need exists for spousal support so it is ordered for a limited time only. Here, all of the aforementioned 13 factors are present except that the length of the marriage was relatively short.
- *Rehabilitative alimony* is designed to facilitate the earning capacity of a dependent spouse. In other words, it provides the economic ability for the spouse to go back to college or get specific job training in order to (re)enter the workforce. Again, this type of alimony is temporary in nature.
- *Permanent alimony* is awarded for life to an economically dependent spouse whose marriage was at least ten years long. The purpose of permanent alimony is to allow the supported spouse to continue living in the lifestyle to which

s/he was accustomed during the marriage, in recognition of the decreased earning potential resulting from staying at home and caring for the house and children. As stated in the foregoing, in New Jersey, the current trend favors limited term alimony over an award of permanent alimony.

As you can see, no clear-cut answer to the question of how long spousal support will need to be paid exists. New Jersey courts seek to create an equitable financial balance based upon what each spouse requires to be financially independent of each other, and not on public assistance. You will have an in-depth series of discussions with your divorce attorney in order to arrive at the best solution for your particular circumstances. Resolving the issue of spousal support may be difficult, but its resolution allows you to move forward and start planning the rest of your life.

c. *How will our assets be divided up? Will we have to sell our house?*

In New Jersey, the division of marital assets is accomplished by what is known as "equitable distribution." This is a legal term which basically means that the property — both real (land, houses, buildings, and the like) and personal (jewelry, mutual funds, stock options, bank and brokerage accounts, retirement assets, small businesses, and so on) — acquired during the marriage is allocated to one or the other spouse in the divorce. Property is not necessarily divided equally, as many factors play into the distribution, including other economic decisions in the divorce like spousal and child support, insurance benefits, debts and liabilities of each person.

Like spousal support, New Jersey lawmakers have enacted laws governing equitable distribution. N.J.S.A. §2A:34-23(h) allows for equitable distribution of real and personal property, and N.J.S.A. §2A:34-23.1 identifies the following 16 factors to be considered in determining how marital assets are to be divided:

(1) The duration of the marriage or civil union;

(2) The age and physical and emotional health of the parties;

(3) The income or property brought to the marriage or civil union by each party;

(4) The standard of living established during the marriage or civil union;

(5) Any written agreement made by the parties before or during the marriage or civil union concerning an arrangement of property distribution;

(6) The economic circumstances of each party at the time the division of property becomes effective;

(7) The income and earning capacity of each party, including educational background, training, employment skills, work experience, length of absence from the job market, custodial responsibilities for children, and the time and expense necessary to acquire sufficient education or training to enable the party to become self-supporting at a standard of living reasonably comparable to that enjoyed during the marriage or civil union;

(8) The contribution by each party to the education, training or earning power of the other;

(9) The contribution of each party to the acquisition, dissipation, preservation, depreciation or appreciation in the amount or value of the marital property, or the property acquired during the marriage or civil union as well as the contributions of a party as a homemaker;

(10) The tax consequences of the proposed distribution to each party;

(11) The present value of the property;

(12) The need of a parent who has physical custody of a child to own or occupy the marital residence and to use or own the household effects;

(13) The debts and liabilities of the parties;

(14) The need for creation, now or in the future, of a trust fund to secure reasonably foreseeable medical or educational costs for a spouse, partner or children;

(15) The extent to which a party deferred achieving their career goals; and

(16) Any other factors that the court may deem relevant.

In general, New Jersey courts approach equitable distribution using a three-step process. First, all of the property that comprises the marital estate is identified. This means that you will discuss with your attorney whether the asset, such as a painting, was purchased during your marriage or brought into the marriage through inheritance or a gift (see the discussion in Myth #1).

Second, once all of the property included in the marital estate is identified, each item is valued. The date of the valuation usually is the date that the complaint of divorce was filed.

Third, the assets are divided between the two parties as fairly as possible. If you, your spouse and the two attorneys are able to come up with a mutual agreement, this is the best possible resolution because you and your spouse will be able to determine who gets which asset. If you cannot work it out, the court will impose a decision for you, and it's not always to the spouses' liking.

Now, let's look at the original question about the possibility of having to sell your house. So many answers to this seemingly simple question exist! You and your former spouse can decide to sell the house and split the proceeds. Or, you can stay in the house and pay your former spouse for his or her half. Or, you can agree to rent out the house if the real estate market is in a slump so you both would be able to realize a higher profit later on. Only your divorce attorney can really guide you as to whether selling your house at this time is the right financial decision for you, or if another, more creative, option is a better resolution in your particular situation.

d. *Will the previously nonworking spouse have to go out and get a job?*

This question is very fact specific and unique to the circumstances surrounding the divorce. In New Jersey, age, length of the marriage, health, prior employment, lifestyle, and the number and ages of children are among the many factors to be considered when making a decision as to the nonworking spouse. In addition, any special needs of the children are also considered, as is the financial situation of the working spouse.

In our discussion about spousal support (Question b. in

this section), "rehabilitative alimony" is discussed. This is a limited-time alimony wherein the economically superior spouse pays for the nonworking spouse to go to college or for other vocational training. However, as discussed, not all situations call for rehabilitative alimony.

Keeping in mind that spousal support may be of limited duration, you should consider your future employment options and goals. You may want to meet with a career counselor/coach to explore your strengths and talents, and develop a strategy to reach your goals. J.K. Rowling only became the famous author of the Harry Potter books after a broken marriage had left her on welfare. You never know where your life will take you!

As oft repeated in this book, you need to consult your divorce attorney in order to determine your options. You may be entitled to permanent alimony but your ex-spouse's financial situation may not allow for an amount that sufficiently covers all of your expenses. You may have a secret desire to pursue a career as a chef, and your divorce may give you the opportunity you need to spread your wings. Only your lawyer will have all of the details at hand to give you a specific answer to this question.

e. What happens if the payor-spouse files for bankruptcy?

In today's economy, unemployment rates in New Jersey are approximately 9.7 percent, and mortgage foreclosures affect about 1 in every 440 housing units. Given these numbers, it is understandable why bankruptcy may be the only option for some people.

But what if your soon-to-be ex-spouse files for bankruptcy? What happens to his or her spousal support and child support obligations? In a word, your ex-spouse CANNOT stop paying child support and spousal support simply because of the bankruptcy filing. When a petition for bankruptcy is filed, the Bankruptcy Code essentially stops all of the debtor's creditors from continuing to collect on their debts. However, the Bankruptcy Code explicitly allows for the continued collection of child and spousal support.

Our discussion does not end there, though. If your former spouse owes back child support or alimony, collection of these debts may, indeed, be stopped by the filing of the bankruptcy petition. You will need to consult with your divorce attorney as to the proper steps under these circumstances.

If one spouse files for bankruptcy protection while you are in the midst of your divorce proceedings, your divorce can still proceed as to the support issues. Distribution of property under equitable distribution will require Bankruptcy Court approval, however. If one spouse is going to file for bankruptcy during your divorce proceedings, your lawyer may or may not recommend that you join in the bankruptcy petition in order to protect yourself. Discuss this possibility with your divorce attorney before taking any legal steps on your own.

Debt accumulated on a joint credit card also is affected by one spouse's filing for bankruptcy. Essentially, if you have a joint credit card and one spouse will not or cannot pay the debt, the credit card company has the right to look for payment of the entire debt from the other spouse. This is true regardless of whether you are the spouse who made the purchase! In your divorce settlement agreement, your attorney should seek to use marital assets to pay off all joint credit card debts in order to try to avoid postdivorce bankruptcy and credit card issues. If this is not possible, your divorce agreement needs to apportion — or allocate — what percentage of the debt is required to be paid off by each spouse. In addition, the wise divorce attorney will include language in the property settlement that covers what happens to the debt in case of one party's ever filing for bankruptcy.

Many more permutations of the bankruptcy scenario play out in New Jersey divorce attorneys' offices every day. In some cases, a bankruptcy that happens after the divorce decree becomes final may be such a change in circumstance as to warrant the modification of a prior support award (called a *Lepis* application, after a landmark New Jersey case). In other cases, motions may have to be made with the Bankruptcy Court. In any bankruptcy situation, or in trying to avoid bankruptcy issues altogether, your divorce attorney will be your guide toward a successful divorce.

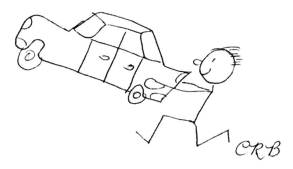

f. Can one spouse get assets held solely in the other spouse's name?

As discussed in Myth #1, the equitable distribution doctrine does not always look to the title of an asset. Rather, the doctrine seeks to divide up property and assets that were acquired during the marriage regardless of which spouse is the legal owner.

Also, as outlined in the answer to Question c. in this section, courts look to sixteen factors when determining how to equitably distribute marital assets. Everything you acquired during your marriage, whether title is held in your name, your spouse's name or jointly, is subject to distribution when you divorce. The only limited exceptions are property or assets that you inherited, those you purchased before your marriage or those that were gifted to you from someone other than your spouse (and the same goes in reverse — if your spouse received a gift from a third party, that asset is not included as marital property). The catch here is that you must have kept this property or asset (or money) separate throughout your marriage. Moreover, if either one of you acquired an asset before your marriage but it increased in value due to direct action or work by the other spouse, that *increase* in value — but *not* the original asset itself — may be considered as marital property subject to equitable distribution.

Under the legal doctrine of equitable distribution, one or the other spouse could be awarded 100 percent of each marital asset, but more commonly the division is about 40 percent to 60 percent per asset. The marital property we're talking about usually includes real estate, cars, stocks, bonds, cash, savings accounts, individual retirement accounts, pensions, 401(k)'s, cash value of life insurance policies, furniture, paintings, timeshares, frequent flier miles and business(es) owned by one or both spouses. This list certainly is not inclusive, but these items are the most common.

This discussion is just the starting point. You must sit down with your divorce attorney and review your financial documentation in order to determine your best course of action. Make sure you tell your lawyer the history of all of your assets, including your bank account balances, *before* you tell your spouse you are filing for divorce. If money mysteriously disappeared from a joint bank account after your spouse learns that you are filing for divorce, you may be entitled to recoup it. The more information your attorney has, the more you will be empowered during your divorce.

g. What should I do if I think my spouse is hiding assets?

Divorce is a stressful time in your life, no doubt about it. No matter what precipitated your current situation, you are in store for some big changes. What you thought you knew about your spouse may no longer be true. Many times, people going through a divorce comment that their former spouse is a stranger to them, despite their having been married for 5, 10, 20 or more years.

One of the most common fears is that a spouse has been squirreling away or hiding assets so that they won't be subject to equitable distribution. This may or may not be true, but you need to do some investigation to be sure.

One step that your divorce attorney may take is to order a title search on your marital home(s). This report will list the owners of the real property and any changes that may have been made of which you may be unaware. The report also will show the open mortgages on the property, including second mortgages or home equity loans or lines of credit. Make sure to review this document carefully to verify that you know about all of the encumbrances on the property and the values agree with your understanding of them. Another type of search you may request is one that shows all real properties held in your spouse's name. The results of this search may uncover some disturbing information, but such information may be very relevant to your divorce and property distribution.

Your divorce attorney will most certainly ask to see your tax returns for the previous five years. A review of these forms will provide a wealth of information about your financial situation, and may help unravel some hidden assets. Of particular note are the line items dealing with interest and dividend income, deductions, capital gains and losses, refunds, and the like. This treasure trove of information may yield clues to unknown possessions.

Depending upon your circumstances, another step your divorce attorney may suggest is that you hire either a private investigator or a forensic accountant. A private investigator can be hired to conduct a financial investigation into your spouse's business(es) and monetary affairs. A forensic accountant is an accountant who is trained to look into suspect accountings in order to gather evidence that can be used in court. Retaining these types of experts may be especially necessary to find assets hidden abroad.

To sum up, the only way the marital estate can be divided properly is if all of the marital assets are known. If you have a feeling that your spouse may be hiding assets, tell that to your divorce attorney, who will know the proper steps to take to try to uncover them. Your lawyer will likely have a ready "team" of experts he or she is used to working with — forensic accountants, private investigators, title search companies, and so forth — and will help you determine if you need the assistance of one or more. In addition, your divorce attorney will suggest language to incorporate into your divorce documents that can protect you if assets magically appear once the divorce is finalized. If you feel protected, you will have the confidence to move on with your life toward a happier future.

2. About children and pets

As a parent, you are responsible for your children's emotional and financial well-being, regardless of whether you and your spouse are living together as a family unit or are divorcing. Your duty as a parent is to guide your child toward becoming a productive, well-adjusted member of society. You and your spouse made the decision to bring children into the marriage, and in "untying" that marriage, you will need to continue to provide love, support and guidance for the children.

Paramount in nearly every divorcing parent's mind is how the separation will impact their children. While assets and money can be replaced, your child's well-being is your most valuable treasure. In some families, emotional attachment to "children" of the four-legged variety runs just as deep. In this section, the seven most commonly asked questions by divorcing couples about children and pets are answered.

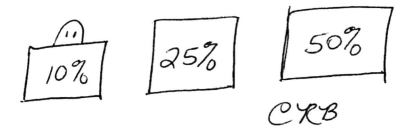

a. *What percentage of my income will I have to pay in child support?*

Before discussing how the amount of child support is determined, the preliminary inquiry is whether child support will be required at all. When deciding whether to make a child support award, New Jersey laws require the courts to consider the following factors:

(1) the needs of the child;

(2) the standard of living and the economic circumstances of each parent;

(3) the sources of income and assets of each parent;

(4) the earning ability of each parent, including educational background, training, employment skills, work experience, custodial responsibility for children (including the cost of providing child care and the length of time and cost of each parent to obtain training and experience for appropriate employment);

(5) the need and capacity of the child for education (including higher education);

(6) the age and health of the child and parents;

(7) the income and earning capacity of the child;

(8) prior support orders for other children;

(9) the reasonable debts and liabilities of each parent and child; and

(10) any other relevant facts.

The purpose of child support is to allow the children of divorced parents to live in the manner to which they were accustomed when the marriage was intact, as much as possible. Children should be able to share in the standard of living of both parents, which is the main motivating factor behind the requirement of child support.

In September 2007, New Jersey established guidelines to aid in determining the amount of child support that must be paid, if any. As with spousal support, the traditional notion that the former husband is always the one paying child support is no longer valid. The breadwinning spouse — husband or wife — will be required to financially support the child(ren) of the marriage. Both parents, however, are responsible for emotionally supporting their children through the stresses of divorce and beyond.

The New Jersey Child Support Guidelines (the "Guidelines") are based on an "income shares concept." This concept apportions between the divorcing parents the average amounts spent on children by intact families, in proportion to each parent's relative income. The Guidelines attempt to allow the children to maintain their lifestyle — shelter, food, clothes, sports, clubs, activities, and so on — as uninterrupted as possible after the divorce. Keep in mind, however, that the Guidelines are just that: guidelines. Your experienced divorce attorney very well may argue for a different amount based upon your particular circumstances.

With this as a backdrop, the Guidelines first divide the spouses' roles into either Sole Parenting or Shared Parenting. In a Sole Parenting situation, the parent that has physical custody of the children generally will receive child support. This is because that parent is providing for the day-to-day needs of the child. On the other hand, in a Shared Parenting situation, where physical custody is roughly equal, the decision as to who pays child support is based upon the parents' respective incomes and amount of time spent with the child.

Each type of parenting, Sole or Shared, has its own worksheet to be completed under the Guidelines. In both worksheets, each parent's net income is computed separately (including spousal support as either income or a deduction, as appropriate), and then a formula is used to determine each parent's percentage share of the family income. From there, certain financial information is entered into the calculations such as health insurance premiums, parenting time expenses, number of the child's overnights with the parent, government benefits for the child, unreimbursed health care expenses, and the like. The worksheets also allow for a Self-Support Reserve Test, to ensure that the payor-spouse's child support obligation does not put him or her into poverty.

The Guidelines do provide a table with specific dollar amounts, per child, that should be paid based upon a weekly income. Before a final child support amount is determined for your particular situation, however, many other calculations are required. Therefore, it does not make sense to include this schedule in this book as it is not such a cut-and-dried exercise.

You now see that to answer the specific question, "What percentage of your income will you have to pay in child support?" requires a great deal of specific calculations. Your divorce attorney will calculate the amount suggested under the Guidelines. Together, you will evaluate whether you feel the amount is appropriate for your children, or if you should deviate from the Guidelines' suggested amount. As an aside, all child support orders are adjusted every two years to reflect an increase in the cost of living, based upon the average change in the Consumer Price Index for New Jersey. You must rely upon your experienced divorce attorney to negotiate the final amount of child support required for your unique circumstance.

CRB

b. *Does the mother automatically get custody of the children?*

In today's society, as has been discussed before, men as well as women often decide to stay home with the children and take care of the household chores. Or, sometimes both parents work outside of the home and provision for day care is made. The antiquated notion that a child belongs with the mother has been replaced by the generally adopted belief that both parents contribute to the well-being of the child.

In addition, "automatically" is not a word often heard in legal circles. Every divorce case is different because every marriage is different, and no sweeping proclamations apply to everyone across the board, *especially* when it comes to child custody.

As earlier discussed in Myth #4, it is New Jersey public policy to assure minor children of frequent and continuing contact with both parents after a divorce. It is, thus, in the public interest to encourage parents to share the rights and responsibilities of child rearing in order to effect this policy. In applying these principles, New Jersey courts look to the "best interests of the child(ren)" when deciding a custody issue. Of paramount consideration is the safety, happiness, physical, mental and moral welfare of the child(ren), with neither parent having a presumed superior right to custody.

New Jersey lawmakers enacted a law, N.J.S.A. § 9:2-4, that lists the following "best interests" factors that go into making a custody determination:

(1) Parents' ability to agree, communicate and cooperate in child-related matters;

(2) Parents' willingness to accept custody and any history of unwillingness to allow visitation not based on substantiated abuse;

(3) Interactions and relationship of the child with its parents and siblings;

(4) History of domestic violence, if any;

(5) Safety of the child and safety of either parent from physical abuse by the other parent;

(6) Preference of the child, when of sufficient age and capacity to reason, so as to form an intelligent decision;

(7) Needs of the child;

(8) Stability of home environment offered by each parent;

(9) Quality and continuity of the child's education;

(10) Fitness of the parents;

(11) Geographic proximity of the parents' homes;

(12) Extent and quality of time spent with a child prior to and subsequent to separation;

(13) Parents' employment responsibilities; and

(14) Number and ages of children.

This list is not exhaustive, and many other considerations can be brought to bear in a custody context. A parent shall not be deemed "unfit," however, unless the parent's conduct has a substantially adverse effect on the child. Make sure to discuss with your divorce attorney any previous alcohol, drug abuse, or domestic violence by your spouse so that all facts are known before a determination is argued.

Moreover, in New Jersey, two types of custody are recognized: physical and legal.

- *Physical (or residential) custody* refers to the parent with whom your child lives on a day-to-day basis, offering physical care and supervision.
- *Legal custody* is the right to make major decisions about your child. These decisions include where your child goes to school, whether your child gets surgery and what kind of religious training your child receives.

Many different permutations of physical and legal custody exist, such as "shared physical and legal custody," "sole physical and shared legal custody," or "sole physical and legal custody." Even where a custody award is made solely to one parent, barring abuse or other dangerous situations, extensive visitation rights usually are incorporated.

Your experienced divorce attorney will discuss your options and offer guidance and negotiation strategies in order to achieve your desired custody outcome. Keeping in mind that a negotiated result is almost always more palatable to both parties than a court-imposed one, it probably will be in your family's best interests to try to work together and create a custody arrangement that reflects both parents' wishes, as well as those of your child(ren).

CRB

c. *Can the custodial parent move out of New Jersey and take my children?*

When you are in the process of discussing custody issues, you must let your divorce attorney know if you, or your soon-to-be former spouse, anticipate moving out of New Jersey, or even the immediate area in which you currently live. Barring consent to relocate, a proposed move could result in a legal custody battle.

Under New Jersey law, children that were either born here or have resided here for at least five years cannot be removed from New Jersey without parental consent or a court order. The reason behind this law is to preserve the rights of the noncustodial parent with his or her child, in order to maintain and develop their familial relationship. If a child is taken out of New Jersey without either consent or an order, criminal sanctions may be imposed, so you don't want to simply take your child with you to your new home in Pennsylvania. You must have this issue ironed out before your move!

If you are contemplating, or have already agreed upon, shared physical and legal custody of your children, the relocation analysis is really a change in custody decision. This decision centers on the best interests of the child, as earlier discussed in Question b.

The analysis is quite different if the arrangement is for sole physical and legal custody, however. Assuming that the custodial parent wants to relocate and the noncustodial parent objects, a judge will have to become involved. This is probably the most difficult decision that a court must make in a divorce proceeding because the judge must do a delicate balancing act. On one hand, the judge is charged with promoting the New Jersey policy of fostering the child's relationship with both parents. On the other hand, the court needs to recognize the rights of the custodial parent to seek a better life for himself or herself, which may be located outside New Jersey.

The court requires that the custodial parent who wants to move show that (1) a good-faith reason exists for the move; (2) the move will not be adverse to the child's best interests; and (3) a visitation schedule has been thought out that will allow the child to maintain a close relationship with the noncustodial parent. The noncustodial parent then must prove why the move is not in the child's best interest, or that it is being proposed in bad faith.

In making a determination about relocation of children by the custodial parent, the following factors are reviewed by a court:

1. Reasons given for the move;
2. Reasons given for opposition;

3. Past history of dealings between the parties insofar as it bears on reasons advanced by both parties for supporting and opposing the move;

4. Whether the child will receive educational, health and leisure opportunities at least equal to what is available in New Jersey;

5. Any special needs or talents of the child that require accommodation;

6. Whether a visitation and communication schedule can be developed that will allow the noncustodial parent to maintain a full and continuous relationship with the child;

7. Likelihood that the custodial parent will continue to foster the child's relationship with the noncustodial parent if the move is allowed;

8. The effect of the move on extended family relationships in New Jersey and in the new location;

9. The child's preference;

10. Whether the child is entering his senior year in high school;

11. Whether the noncustodial parent has the ability to relocate to the new location; and

12. Any other factor bearing upon the child's best interests.

As you can see, this is an intensely fact-driven argument — for or against the custodial parent moving out of the area and taking the children. Your experienced divorce attorney will review all of the many factors with you so that your rights as a parent are protected. Because your child is your most valuable treasure, and emotions run very high on this extremely hot-button issue, you will need to rely upon your lawyer's guidance in order to have a successful outcome.

d. *Can the payor-spouse quit a job and take a lower-paying one in order to reduce child support and alimony payments?*

In a word, no.

New Jersey courts do not allow a payor-spouse to willfully quit a job and deliberately take a lower-paying one in order to reduce child support or spousal payments. Nor can the payor-spouse retire for the purpose of evading paying spousal and/or child support.

If you suspect your spouse is voluntarily remaining unemployed or underemployed, your divorce attorney will object to any request by the spouse to reduce the support award. If the court agrees with you, then the judge will "impute income" to your ex-spouse. This means that the court will estimate how much a person with similar earning capacity, work history, job qualifications, educational background, potential employment and regional opportunities should be earning. The same holds true regarding "imputing income" if no support amount has been awarded yet in your divorce proceeding.

However, given today's economic climate, and nearly double-digit unemployment in New Jersey, many people are unemployed or underemployed. Support orders entered earlier may have become impossible to fulfill if the payor-spouse is not employed. In such a case, the court allows for that spouse to file a *Lepis* motion, as it is called after a landmark case in family law, to prove a "substantial change in circumstances."

The party making a *Lepis* motion to request a decrease in support payments must prove that the lowered income is permanent. Moreover, it must be proven that after many attempts, an equivalent paying job could not be obtained. The proofs needed are very detailed such as e-mails, letters, termination notices, interview calendars, and the like. Your divorce attorney will be involved in guiding you through this rather detailed process, to evaluate the proofs and assist you in properly opposing or filing the motion. In addition, it is not uncommon for a court to temporarily grant a reduction in support, and then revisit it again in six months.

When crafting your divorce settlement agreement, your lawyer may discuss an "*anti-Lepis* clause." This means that, although allowed, both parties agree to waive the right to go back to the Court and make a *Lepis* motion. Your experienced divorce attorney will weigh the pros and cons of including this clause in your agreement, and the possible ramifications. One of the more important consequences of an *anti-Lepis* clause is that you may avert a possible continuous cycle of re-litigating your divorce. New Jersey courts are divided, however, on the enforceability of such clauses, so you must have a full discussion with your lawyer to understand all of your options, and be able to confidently move forward with the next chapter of your life.

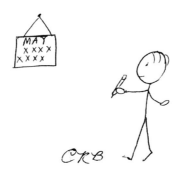

CRB

e. *How long will the payor-spouse have to pay child support?*
Believe it or not, no simple answer exists for this question.
Many people think that when a child turns 18, child support
automatically stops. In truth, child support may end before or
well after your son or daughter graduates from high school. If
no application is made to the court, child support ends when the
"child" turns 26!

In New Jersey, parents — whether biological or via
adoption — are required to pay child support until their child is
"emancipated." "Emancipated" means when the child (of any
age) has demonstrated freedom from parental control or support
and an ability to be self-supporting. It is essentially when the
dependent role of parent and child is concluded.

Emancipation *may* occur when the child reaches the age of
majority (18), or goes on active military duty, or gets married/
has a baby, or obtains full-time employment. Additionally,
emancipation automatically is granted if the parents' rights and
responsibilities are legally terminated, such as by adoption. If
your child has special needs or is in college, however, a child
support obligation may continue longer. Once again, the
determination of emancipation is extremely fact-driven. Your
divorce attorney will be able to offer you guidance as to when it
would be appropriate to seek a court order of emancipation and
end your child support obligation.

Moreover, in New Jersey, the courts strongly favor ongoing education and generally require that parents pay for their child's college tuition, if they are financially able. In this situation, child support, *per se*, may end and/or be replaced with an obligation to pay for college. The criteria used to determine whether a parent will have to pay for his or her child's college expenses are as follows:

(1) the effect of the background, values and goals of the parent on the reasonableness of the expectation of the child for higher education;

(2) the amount of contribution sought by the child for the cost of the higher education;

(3) the ability of the parent to pay that cost;

(4) the relationship of the requested contribution to the kind of school or course of study sought by the child;

(5) the financial resources of both parties;

(6) the commitment to and aptitude of the child for the requested education;

(7) the financial resources of the child, including assets held individually or in custodianship or trust;

(8) the ability of the child to earn income during the school year or on vacation;

(9) the availability of financial aid in the form of college grants;

(10) the child's relationship to the paying parent, including mutual affection and shared goals as well as responsiveness to parental advice and guidance; and

(11) the relationship of education requested to any prior training and to the overall long-range goals of the child.

When negotiating your property settlement agreement, a.k.a. final divorce agreement, your experienced divorce attorney may include a provision that outlines the circumstances or events that will trigger the end of child support. Keep in mind, however, that child support actually is the child's right, and cannot be summarily negotiated away by the parents.

Procedurally, when you know that the circumstances requiring child support will be ending, an application to the court will need to be filed in order to legally declare your child emancipated. Then, and only then, will your child support obligation be terminated. As you can see, you may be forging a very long-term relationship with your divorce attorney, so selection of a qualified and compatible lawyer from the onset is very advantageous.

f. *Will I only get to see my children every other weekend?*

New Jersey recognizes a constitutional right for a parent to see his or her children. This right will only be terminated if it is proven that the parent would cause physical and/or emotional harm to the child, and that no other alternatives to termination exist.

Child visitation plans are as plentiful as there are divorced couples with children. Your experienced divorce attorney will help you craft an appropriate plan suitable for your life and work schedule. A typical visitation schedule is for the children to spend every other weekend (from Friday at 6 p.m. until Sunday at 6 p.m.) and every Wednesday evening (from 6 p.m. until 9 p.m.) with the noncustodial parent. However, this is not etched in stone, and you are free to develop your own plan. If parents are unable to reach an amicable child visitation solution, New Jersey courts will impose one, but — as with most things — it is better to mutually agree upon a plan.

When you and your divorce attorney are sitting down to discuss a visitation schedule, you need to be cognizant of your lifestyle — if your work hours are 8 a.m. until 8 p.m. Monday through Friday, you wouldn't want to schedule visitation with your preschool-aged children during the afternoons. In addition, keep in mind the timing for any activities or sports in which your children are involved, summer months, holidays and family obligations, and make the appropriate arrangements for them. For example, every Mother's Day will be spent with the mother, regardless of whether it's "her" weekend, and the same holds true for Father's Day. Also, if you have a timeshare for a week during spring break, build that into your visitation plan. Thanksgiving may be celebrated with each parent on alternating years. By planning ahead for most foreseeable contingencies, you will have already ironed out some of the sticky details with your former spouse — with the help of lawyers — and many conflicts down the road will be avoided.

One of the key elements in any visitation plan is flexibility. If your spouse's parents are in town from Florida and she asks for some extra time with the children, try to be amenable if the change fits in your schedule. More than likely, you may want a couple of extra hours with your children down the road and your kindness should be remembered. You catch more bees with honey. Why be spiteful? It is your children who suffer the most.

Of course, if your former spouse was physically or emotionally abusive during your marriage, or a drug abuser or alcoholic, New Jersey allows for limited, supervised visitation.

In the case of supervised visitation with your children, the meetings may take place in a local sheriff's office or, more often, under the supervision of a person approved by the court. Make sure you inform your lawyer about any such issues, as they can have a major impact on your entire divorce proceedings.

The point of a visitation schedule is to allow your children to spend quality time with each parent. After all, New Jersey courts recognize that it is in the best interests of the child, in most cases, to receive the benefit of both parents' wisdom and guidance. With this in mind, when your child returns from your former spouse's house, do not use the time to "debrief" him about your ex's new life. It certainly is acceptable to ask about what activities your child did, but he is not your spy and should not be put in an untenable situation. A successful divorce means that each spouse has closed the door on the marriage but they are working together as mature adults to raise their children. Your experienced divorce attorney will discuss potential roadblocks and offer solutions before you enter into a binding visitation schedule.

g. *Who gets custody of our pets?*

Custody issues can arise not only around children, but concerning the four-legged and furry members of your family as well. After all, dogs, cats and other animals kept as pets provide companionship and contribute to their owners' overall emotional well-being. When you are getting a divorce, custody of your pet may be another major issue to be determined, so make sure your divorce attorney is apprised of any family pets.

This very issue was addressed in a 2009 landmark decision in New Jersey. The court set a new standard for deciding who gets custody of a pet based upon "sincere affection for and attachment to" the animal. In declining to adopt a "best interests of the pet" standard, the court stated that it was "less confident that there are judicially discoverable and manageable standards for resolving questions of possession from the perspective of a pet, at least apart from cases involving abuse or neglect contrary to public policies expressed in laws designed to protect animals."

In that case, the New Jersey court found that pets are a unique form of property that elicit sentimental attachment and have a special subjective value. In determining who should be awarded custody of the family pet, the court may consider which party has paid attention to the animal's basic daily needs such as food, shelter, physical care, exercise and grooming. In addition, deference should be allocated to the person who takes the pet to the veterinarian, provides for social interactions (as appropriate), assures that state and local regulations are met and has the greatest ability to financially support the pet.

Now, the goal of a successful divorce is to be able, amicably, to decide your own fate, reach closure and move forward with your new life. Knowing what factors courts in New Jersey review in order to make a pet custody decision should enable you to reach an agreement without needing court intervention. As discussed previously, revenge is not the goal here, so if you know your soon-to-be former spouse is deeply attached to your family dog, do not use Eli or Chloe as a weapon for spite.

Many property settlement agreements include provisions for the family pet. Again, you can be as creative in your arrangements as you would like. Shared custody, visitation and decisions about medical treatments all can be included in your divorce agreement. For example, your cat, Mr. Whiskers, can have primary residence with you but spend every other weekend with your former spouse and all veterinarian visits have to be attended by both of you.

While this question may sound funny to some, pet custody issues are extremely important to animal lovers. Unlike personal property items like a painting or even the house, you cannot simply have one spouse keep the ferret and pay the other its purchase price. A pet becomes a part of the family — offering love and companionship — and, therefore, has special treatment in the New Jersey courts. Your experienced divorce attorney will guide you through this emotional issue, offering creative solutions that will enable you to maintain your relationship with your pet well after your divorce is final.

3. **About the process**

As with many people, getting a divorce may be the first time you've set foot into the legal arena. Sure, you've seen trials on television, but you may not have any first-hand legal experience outside of fighting a traffic ticket in municipal court. You may have heard horror stories about people feeling bamboozled in court, or you're just plain scared of being ridiculed by a "Judge Judy."

The divorce process, especially at the beginning stages, is emotionally overwhelming. These feelings can be compounded by dealing with unknown legal procedures. In this section of the book, the seven most frequently asked questions about the legal process of getting divorced in New Jersey are answered.

a. *How long before I'll be divorced?*

Once you've made the decision that you want to divorce your spouse, most people just want it to be over and done with. Right away. NOW!

Prior to January 20, 2007, the "no fault" grounds for divorce in New Jersey required that a divorcing couple live separate and apart for eighteen months before being eligible to file for divorce. However, on January 20, 2007, the New Jersey legislature added another "no fault" ground for divorce, as follows: There must be irreconcilable differences that have lasted for a period of at least six months, and have led to a breakdown of the marriage, for which there is no reasonable prospect of reconciliation. This change in the law was significant, because now the person filing for divorce need only allege irreconcilable differences for six months, rather than living apart for eighteen months, thereby cutting down the length of time required to get a divorce by at least one year.

Even with this new "no fault" ground, however, the legal process does not run on a very quick timetable. There are certain rules and procedures that need to be followed that take time to complete. In general, New Jersey courts seek to finalize a divorce in about one year, but it may take much longer or shorter depending upon your particular circumstances.

You see, the two parts of a divorce that the law needs to address are grounds and distribution/children/support. Assuming that you file under the six-month "no fault" irreconcilable difference ground, the first part is quickly satisfied. In most divorce cases, this "no fault" ground is the norm now in New Jersey. However, when other grounds are alleged, such as adultery, extreme cruelty or addiction, your spouse may argue with you as to the grounds (called "contesting") and extend the time it takes for your divorce to get past this first hurdle.

The second part that needs to be addressed in order to get a divorce in New Jersey is the dividing up of assets, attending to the needs of the children and deciding upon the amount of support. This is when most divorces slow down. First, custody and visitation need to be ironed out (for much more information about this subject, review the preceding discussion in Section 2). Once issues surrounding the children are decided, child and spousal support as well as property distribution need to be agreed upon (for information about these subjects, see Sections 1 and 2). As you can well imagine, these emotional and financial issues can easily become complex and cause battle lines to be drawn. Your experienced divorce attorney will help you navigate all of these issues as swiftly as possible, but not so swiftly as to gloss over important details of your case.

If you and your spouse have only been married for two years, you live in a rental apartment and have no children, your divorce proceedings may be relatively quick. However, if you have a beloved dog, visitation and/or custody issues may take some time to be agreed upon and documented. Now, suppose you have been married for 12 years, own a home and some other assets, and have two children ages five and seven. In order to divide up all of your assets, you and your spouse will need to compile a complete list of assets and agree upon their distribution. Moreover, custody and visitation schedules need to be determined as to your children, and child and spousal support set. Even in the most amicable situations, attending to small children's needs and the division of marital assets take time. If emotions are running high, this process will take much longer as "cooling off" periods may be required to reach agreements on all of these issues. The length of time to reach a final divorce will be extended even further if the spouses simply cannot agree and need judicial intervention.

Your experienced divorce attorney will be there with you every step of the way, guiding you toward your ultimate goal of a successful divorce. Being able to reach an agreement with your soon-to-be former spouse certainly will move the proceedings along more quickly, usually resulting in a more acceptable resolution. As most people feel out of control, somewhat, when going through a divorce, being able to determine your own outcome by agreement helps in the healing process as well. A word of caution: You should not agree to something simply for the sake of speeding up your divorce and "getting it over with." Your lawyer will advise you of all your options and you should weigh the advice carefully. After all, it is much more advantageous to be divorced and satisfied with all of your decisions than just to be divorced quickly.

b. How expensive is it to get divorced? Will the higher-earning spouse be required to pay all legal fees?

As you can probably guess, no definitive answer exists to the question of "how expensive is it to get divorced?" Lawyers charge an hourly rate to represent you in your divorce, so the amount of legal fees you will need to pay is directly related to the length of time it takes to resolve all of your specific issues. With very few exceptions, no lawyer does a divorce on a flat fee basis due to unexpected twists and turns that can arise in any divorce matter. It is also not permitted for a lawyer in New Jersey to take on a divorce case on a contingency fee basis.

When you meet with your prospective divorce attorney for your initial consultation, usually a free meeting, he or she will discuss the hourly rate and the amount of retainer required. A retainer is a lump sum you pay up front to the attorney, which is drawn down on on a monthly basis according to the number of hours incurred that month. When the retainer dips to a certain, specified level, your lawyer will ask that it be replenished. Make sure that you receive full and explicit instructions as to the attorney's fees and retainer requirements, and that you are comfortable with them before signing a retainer letter. If you don't "click" with the attorney, or feel he or she is being shady in any way about fees or retainers, thank him for the initial consultation and set up another appointment with a new lawyer. Because you will be working together during a difficult time, and sharing very personal information, you must be comfortable with your choice of attorney.

Even if you and your spouse believe you have worked out all of the issues prior to filing for divorce, it is highly recommended that you retain an attorney to represent you. In such a case, the lawyer will spend minimal time with you but will review all of the documents to ensure that all the legalities are met and you are properly protected going forward. There's an old adage that you should remember: "He who represents himself has a fool for a client." Moreover, one attorney cannot represent both parties in a divorce due to ethical restrictions.

In addition to paying your divorce attorney for the time he or she spends working on your case, you need to be aware that there are other fees and costs associated with getting a divorce in New Jersey. When you file certain papers in the court, a filing fee is required. At the present time, filing fees can range from $30 to over $200, depending upon the type of document you are filing. The court also requires that each party to a divorce where children are involved take a Parent Education Class, the fee for which is $30 currently. As an aside, the court is very strict about your attending the Parent Education Class. If you choose to skip it, you are opening yourself up to possible sanctions and negative results in your custody decision. Your experienced divorce attorney will be able to tell you any filing fees and will keep you apprised of the Parent Education Class enrollment.

Other costs may also be incurred in your divorce litigation in addition to legal fees. If your case goes into a "discovery" phase (more on that in Section d, which follows next), fees associated with taking a deposition and copying documents may arise. Depending upon the complexity of your situation and whether you are able to resolve your issues by agreement, experts may need to be brought in. These experts can include forensic accountants, private investigators, child custody evaluators, pension appraisers and employment analysts, among others. Before you are charged with any costs, your divorce lawyer will let you know their approximate total fees. You must give your prior approval before any experts are hired. Remember, this is your divorce and you are in charge — your divorce attorney is just your knowledgeable guide.

Now, if you're thinking to yourself that you cannot afford to pay a lawyer's fees and costs, don't despair. Divorce is one exception to the general rule that in America each party to a lawsuit is required to pay his or her own attorney's fees. If both spouses can afford to pay their own attorney's fees, this issue is moot. However, if an inequality of financial resources resulting from the impending divorce exists, you can still retain a divorce attorney and ask your soon-to-be former spouse to pay the bill. In such a situation, the financially dependent spouse will need to make an application to the court for attorney's fees to be paid by the other spouse. In making this determination, the court will look at the reasonableness and good faith of the positions advanced by the parties as well as financial circumstances. The attorney's fees award may be made during the pendency of the divorce proceedings or at their conclusion. Your experienced divorce attorney will be able to discuss this issue with you during your initial consultation and explain all of your options.

c. *Will I have to go to trial to get divorced?*

As earlier discussed, when we talked about the 7 Myths about Divorce, it is unlikely that your divorce will have to be decided at trial. Only 10 percent of all New Jersey divorces are resolved through an actual trial. This is not to say that you won't have to appear before a family court judge and possibly even give testimony on an issue in your case, as avoiding a courtroom altogether when seeking a divorce is unlikely.

As often repeated throughout this book, the best results in a divorce are those agreed upon by the parties themselves. Think about it, when you were a child, were you happier when you and your sibling got into an argument and came to a resolution on your own, or when one of your parents stepped in and "laid down the law"?

Many layers are built into New Jersey's court system to allow parties seeking a divorce to avoid a trial and speedily resolve their issues. First, the law favors settlements, so if you and your former spouse can work out your issues amicably, your case will end there. If you cannot agree on a resolution, your divorce attorney will speak directly with your spouse's lawyer to try to work out the sticking points. If you have open issues regarding custody and/or parenting time, a judge will send your case to mandatory mediation soon after your case is filed. Failing resolution with these attempts, you may choose to go to a mediator or arbitrator to help resolve your disputes (see Myth #5, in the previous chapter).

The next step in the divorce process, should you get this far, is a Matrimonial Early Settlement Panel ("MESP"), which is run by the court system. With a MESP, instead of being heard by a judge, your case will be heard by a panel of volunteer family law attorneys. The result of a MESP is that the panel makes a set of recommendations about how your issues should be resolved. If you and your spouse accept the panel's recommendations, or agree upon modified recommendations, in most circumstances you bring them to the judge in the courtroom, and your divorce can then be obtained on that day.

If, after all of these layers, you and your soon-to-be former spouse still are unable to find common ground regarding monetary issues, a judge will send your case to mandatory financial mediation. Thereafter, failing resolution of your divorce issues, you will be ordered to attend an Intensive

Settlement Conference Day where you, your spouse and both divorce attorneys will meet with the judge and try to iron out the remaining details. Once you have exhausted all of these many layers without being able to settle your differences, then — and only then — your case will be set for trial. In New Jersey, your case will be heard at what's called a "bench trial," meaning that the decision will be made by a judge, not a jury.

For many reasons, a trial is the least appealing way to finalize a divorce. There is the increased length of time, expenses for legal and experts' fees, and the inability to control the outcome. From the outset, your divorce attorney will outline all of the options for resolving your issues. Then, as your case progresses, he or she will guide you to the appropriate mechanisms for reaching the right resolution for you. Your experienced lawyer will take the time necessary to prepare you if and when you need to testify in court, whether it be at trial or a hearing on a motion. Working together, you ultimately will achieve your desired result: a new beginning.

d.   What legal papers should I expect to be filed in court?

Now that you've made the difficult decision to end your marriage, and understand that you need to hire an experienced divorce attorney to guide you, many people next wonder about exactly what the legal process entails. This section describes, in general, the types of legal documents that are filed with a court in the majority of divorce proceedings. Of course, your case may require different papers or have them filed in a different order, so you need to rely upon the guidance of your lawyer who will be intimately familiar with your particular facts and circumstances.

To start the divorce process, the first legal document filed in court is called a "Complaint for Divorce." Together with a Case Information Statement, Insurance Certification, Confidential Litigant Information Sheet and filing fee, the Complaint begins your case for divorce. The Complaint states the cause of action — the ground(s) upon which you are suing for divorce — and gives a brief synopsis of the facts plus the names and addresses of the divorcing spouses and any children, in separately numbered paragraphs. The Complaint will be filed in the Superior Court of New Jersey, Chancery Division, Family Part, in the county in which you reside (check out Section e, which follows next, for more information about "jurisdiction"). The person filing the Complaint is called the "plaintiff" or "petitioner."

After your Complaint is filed, it will receive a docket number from the court, which is just a number assigned to your particular case for identification purposes. The Complaint then will be returned to your attorney for service on your soon-to-be former spouse. Service can be effectuated via consent by having your spouse or his/her attorney sign an Acknowledgment of Service, or if necessary it can be served through a process server: "Are you Mrs. Smith? (Hands over an envelope) You've been served!"

Following service of the Complaint, your spouse will have 35 days to file an Answer and/or Counterclaim or a simple Appearance. Don't be dismayed if your spouse's attorney calls your lawyer and asks for an extension of time to answer the Complaint. These requests normally are granted out of professional courtesy. In the Answer, responses to each of the numbered paragraphs in the Complaint are made, together with any separate, affirmative defenses. The person filing the Answer is called the "defendant" or "respondent." If a "Counterclaim" is added to the Answer, which is a complaint the defendant brings, the petitioner will then have 20 days to file an Answer to the Counterclaim. Should no Answer or Appearance be filed to the Complaint, your lawyer will proceed to seek a "Default Judgment."

Given that New Jersey now recognizes a "no fault" divorce — meaning that the grounds for filing a Complaint simply can be irreconcilable differences for six months — it is not critical which spouse is the plaintiff and which spouse is the defendant. So, if you are served with a Complaint, do not feel as if you are somehow at a disadvantage because you are not the "plaintiff." Your experienced divorce attorney will discuss the appropriate strategy for your individual situation.

Within 20 days of the filing of the last pleading, both parties are required to file a Case Information Statement, which is a certified statement disclosing all the financial information of the marriage including income, assets and liabilities. This helps the court to determine the lifestyle of the marriage and the issues that need to be addressed in your particular divorce. In 30 days or so after an Answer and/or Answer to Counterclaim is filed, the plaintiff and defendant will attend a Parent Education Class. Meanwhile, the parties' attorneys will attend a Case Management Conference and put together a Case Management Order, which outlines all the important deadlines until trial.

The next step in the divorce litigation is called "discovery." This phase of your case entails papers called Interrogatories, Document Demands and Requests for Admissions. Each side can serve the other side with any or all of these discovery methods, or can also serve nonparties via subpoena, with responses generally due within 30 days. "Interrogatories" are a list of questions that one side wants the other to respond to, in writing, via a document called "Answers to Interrogatories." Your attorney will ask you to review the questions and give him or her your responses, and then work with you to put your answers into the proper format. "Document Demands" are just that: requests for documents. Your lawyer will send you the "Document Demands" and ask you to review your papers for any documents that are responsive to them. When you give the documents to your lawyer, he or she will review them and configure them correctly to give them over to the other side. "Requests for Admissions" are a list of statements that require you, via your attorney, to either respond in writing with "admit" or "deny." Your lawyer will assist you every step of the way, so don't feel as if you are on your own with these discovery demands.

A "Notice of Deposition" is another discovery method. A deposition is where a person is asked questions by the attorney, in front of a court reporter who transcribes every word. For example, the soon-to-be former wife will receive a "Notice of Deposition." The husband's attorney will ask the questions, usually in a conference room in his office. The wife's attorney will be present for the deposition and will raise any necessary objections. Before your deposition, your attorney will sit with you to prepare you for the types of questions that most likely will be asked. That way, you are confident and feel comfortable at your deposition. After the deposition, you will pay for and receive a transcript from the court reporter. Depositions are not limited to just the plaintiff or defendant, as anyone with information relevant to the divorce can be summoned for one. Usually, however, children are not deposed, so you shouldn't worry about their being drawn into a deposition.

Another document that you probably will come across is a "Motion." A motion is simply a formal request to the judge for specific consideration about an issue — a letter will not suffice. Issues that may lead to motion practice concern payment of support, children/visitation/parenting, payment of certain bills or any other conflict that the parties are unable to resolve on their own. The Motion is accompanied by a "Notice of Motion" which lets the other side know when the court will have a hearing on the request and gives other deadlines, such as when objections are due. After the hearing, the judge will issue an Order ruling on the motion. Motions may be brought during the pendency of your divorce case, or after it is completed if changes need to be addressed. Your experienced divorce attorney will know when a motion is appropriate and will guide you through the legal procedures.

The document legally ending your marriage is called a "Judgment of Divorce," which is an Order signed by the judge. In the Judgment of Divorce, your marriage is officially dissolved, and the wife is permitted to resume her maiden name if she chooses to. As discussed in this book, the parties usually work out their own agreement rather than go to trial, which results in a "Marital Settlement Agreement" (sometimes called a "Property Settlement Agreement"). All of the parties' rights and obligations, including division of property and assets, child custody and support agreements, are memorialized in this document. As with every step of your case, your divorce lawyer will make sure all of your rights are protected before you sign on the dotted line and close this chapter of your life.

e. Can I get a divorce in NJ if we weren't married in this state?

Nowadays in America, it is unusual for a person to be born, marry and reside in just one state. It is much more common for someone to move among several states during his or her lifetime. In many cases, couples marry in the hometown of the bride, or in the Wedding Capital of the World, Las Vegas. With the rise of destination weddings, more commonly marriages are taking place outside of the United States as well. So, what if you were married outside of New Jersey, or even in a foreign country? Can you still get a divorce in New Jersey?

The answer to this question is a qualified yes. In general, if you have lived in New Jersey for at least one year, you will have met the residency qualifications to file for divorce here. So long as one party to the divorce action has been a NJ resident for the minimum 12-month time frame, the New Jersey courts have what is called in the legal world "jurisdiction" and can rule on your case. You do not, however, have to have lived in the same house for this entire period and can have moved within the state. So, the location of your wedding ceremony, be it New Jersey, Nevada or the Dominican Republic, is not a determinative factor.

If your spouse lives in another state, but you have lived here for more than one year, you still can go to the New Jersey courts for your divorce. The process for serving the Complaint will be a bit more complicated, but your experienced divorce attorney should be able to handle this without too much difficulty. Moreover, if the non-NJ spouse files an Answer in the case, the court will be deemed to have jurisdiction. After the divorce case is filed, you and/or your spouse are free to move out of the state, but keep in mind that you will have to return for any hearings, conferences, and other legal meetings as well as to see your children.

The Superior Court system within New Jersey is divided up based upon counties. Therefore, when you file for divorce, you do so in the county in which you or your spouse lives, called the "venue." The plaintiff gets to choose in which county to file (usually closest to his or her home). This is one slight advantage of being the party filing the Complaint — mileage costs can add up.

When you have your initial consultation with your divorce lawyer, make sure to let him know about your living arrangements over the past year. So long as you have been living in New Jersey for the past year, jurisdiction should not be an issue with your case. Also, tell him where you were married, in case any documentation has to be obtained from that location. If you or your spouse are considering moving out of state, make sure to discuss those intentions with your attorney. Providing this information to your legal representative will ensure as smooth a navigation of the legal waters as is possible. After all, your ultimate goal is a successful divorce, which includes careful planning.

CRB

f. If my spouse abuses me, what can I do?

Domestic violence seems to be on the rise, as witnessed by the number of stories in newspapers and on television. Nearly every week, a story makes the headlines about a fight between former spouses resulting in a trip to the hospital. If you feel that your life, or the lives of your children, are in danger from your spouse, *immediate action* must be taken.

The first step is to tell your divorce attorney of any abuse. In New Jersey, the legislature enacted a law, the "Prevention of Domestic Violence Act," that allows one spouse to get a restraining order and/or file a criminal complaint against the other if being subjected to assault, sexual assault, harassment, stalking or other acts of cruelty. Specifically, the Prevention of Domestic Violence Act lists the following as acts as domestic violence when perpetrated by one spouse on the other: assault, burglary, criminal mischief, criminal restraint, terroristic threats, criminal sexual contact, criminal trespass, false imprisonment, harassment, homicide, kidnapping, lewdness, sexual assault, or stalking. If you feel threatened by your spouse, let your lawyer know right away. Whether this violence has been a pattern during your relationship or has just surfaced in the face of your divorce, no one should ever live in fear.

If you are the victim of abuse, your lawyer may recommend that you file a civil complaint for domestic violence, which seeks to protect you from your abuser. As soon as an incident of abuse occurs, you must see a doctor (if your injuries warrant) and/or get your injuries documented via photographs. Then, you will file a complaint with the court; this is the same court in which your divorce case is pending. If the incident occurs outside of the Court's business hours, you may file your complaint with the police, who will contact a Municipal Court judge.

With either route, your case will be heard right away and an "*Ex Parte* Temporary Restraining Order" may be issued if the judge feels that imminent danger of domestic violence exists. "*Ex parte*" simply means that one side is going to the court without having the other side present. Because of the nature of domestic violence cases, and the swiftness in which they are brought before a judge, the proceedings are usually *ex parte* at the beginning. A "temporary restraining order," or "TRO," sets specific limits on the contact your abuser/spouse is allowed to have with you until another hearing is set, called the "Domestic Violence Hearing," usually 10 days later.

The limitations contained in a TRO may include forbidding your abuser/spouse (1) from coming within a certain geographic area of you and/or your children or contacting you in person, via telephone or in writing; (2) from possessing any firearms or other weapons; (3) from committing any other acts of domestic violence; or (4) any other appropriate restrictions. When you receive a TRO, your attorney will advise you to make several copies and keep one with you at all times. Once a TRO is issued by a judge, the document will be personally served upon your abuser/spouse by the police department.

Approximately 10 days after a TRO is issued, both you and your abuser/spouse will be required to attend the Domestic Violence Hearing. You both will be able to bring witnesses to testify about the incident. Your divorce attorney will guide you through this process and ease your nerves about confronting your abuser. Just make sure to tell the judge exactly what happened, truthfully. If the judge determines that an act of domestic violence occurred, the abuser/spouse may be subjected to a fine. In addition, pursuant to the Prevention of Domestic Violence Act, the judge also may issue an "Order of Protection" that will list the exact conditions that your abuser must satisfy. The Order of Protection will last forever unless dismissed by the victim.

The conditions that may be imposed on your abuser/spouse in an Order of Protection will be tailored to your particular situation. Your Order of Protection may include some or all of these conditions:

1. Restraining the abuser from any further acts of domestic violence against you;

2. Preventing the abuser from possessing firearms or weapons and/or ordering the search and seizure of any weapons;

3. Requiring that your abuser leave the marital home, regardless of who has title;

4. Removing all personal belongings, with police supervision, from all properties — residential or business — shared with you;

5. Prohibiting the abuser from entering your residence, property, school and/or place of employment;

6. Turning over custody of the children to you;

7. Severely limiting or eliminating parenting time, or ordering supervised visitation only;

8. Preventing any contact with you or your children, either directly or through third parties, in person, in writing or over the telephone;

9. Paying for your costs that resulted from the domestic violence, including medical/dental treatment, moving

expenses, loss of earnings, as well as for those expenses suffered by other people that helped you or got hurt by the abuser, including your attorney's fees and other damages;

10. Requiring the abuser to continue to make rent or mortgage payments and pay other household bills;

11. Ordering the abuser to pay, or to continue to pay, child and spousal support;

12. Requiring the abuser to attend domestic violence counseling, anger management classes, AA or NA;

13. Ordering a psychiatric evaluation of the abuser; and/or

14. Any other appropriate relief for you and your children.

As with the TRO, your divorce lawyer will instruct you to make several copies of the Order of Protection, and to always carry one with you. You should keep a copy of the Order of Protection at your home, your office and in your purse, plus provide a copy to a trusted neighbor, relative, babysitter/day care and the police departments in the locations where you live and work. You also would be well advised to carry a cell phone that is charged at all times, just in case your abuser/spouse violates the terms of the Final Order and you need to contact either the police, a friend or your lawyer. Another note of caution: Prudence dictates that you change both your locks and your telephone number. It is better to be safe than sorry.

Sadly, even after an Order of Protection is entered by the court, your abuser/spouse may violate its terms. If the violation is failure to return personal property, failure to pay support or rent, not complying with custody or visitation conditions, or failing to attend domestic violence counseling, you should call the Family Court Domestic Violence Unit and they will enforce the Order. *For all other violations, immediately call the police.* Your abuser/spouse will be arrested and may be subject to jail time.

In many cases after a TRO is issued, your divorce attorney may suggest that you and your spouse discuss the possibility of entering into a "Consent Order." A Consent Order contains essentially the same terms and restrictions as an Order of Protection, but is agreed upon by both parties and does not carry a criminal penalty should it be violated. In situations where the parties are attempting to resolve their differences as amicably as possible, a Consent Order may provide the security needed while allowing for continued negotiations as to the distribution of property, assets and childcare.

In addition to filing a civil complaint and receiving an Order of Protection, you also may file a criminal complaint against your abuser/spouse. The purpose of filing a criminal complaint for domestic violence is to punish your abuser; you are not the plaintiff in a criminal case, the State of New Jersey, via the prosecutor, is. Your experienced divorce attorney will advise you to go, and perhaps accompany you, to the police department or municipal court in the town in which the violence occurred in order to file your criminal complaint. You will be asked for the exact details of the incident as well as for evidence of the abuse, so photographs or notes from the doctor who treated you are helpful. Depending upon the town, a warrant for your abuser's arrest will be made out, or a summons issued. Your abuser/spouse will be brought before a judge and bail set. Bail may or may not include payment of money or a bond, and usually is accompanied by a set of restrictions pending a final hearing. Also, depending upon your town and the severity of the charges, the criminal case will go through the municipal court system or be turned over to the prosecutor's office. The final result of a criminal complaint is jail time, if the case is proven beyond a reasonable doubt.

As a side note, your divorce lawyer will advise you that both parties to the divorce should stay in the marital residence until such time as your divorce is final or a specific agreement about living arrangements is made. The one exception to this general rule, however, is when domestic violence is present. In cases of domestic violence, as we have just discussed, the abuser will be excluded from the home immediately.

Domestic violence is a very serious issue, which can quickly escalate and become deadly. If you are in need of help, the Office of the Attorney General's website identifies every county in New Jersey and its Domestic Violence Program. Do not hesitate to reach out for assistance for yourself and your children if you are a victim of domestic violence. Your experienced divorce attorney will help you with the legal end of obtaining a TRO and Order of Protection as well as filing a criminal complaint, but he or she is no substitute for a licensed professional in the domestic violence arena. Remember too that not only husbands are the abusers — wives have been known to physically abuse and threaten their husbands as well.

g. What if I don't like a judge's decision about custody, visitation, support or equitable distribution?

The good news: If the judge makes a ruling in your divorce case that you think is unfair or incorrect, you may have an opportunity to, essentially, go over the judge's head and file an appeal with the Appellate Division. And if you don't like the result from the Appellate Division, one more level of appeal exists: to the Supreme Court of New Jersey.

The bad news: Filing an appeal costs both time and money. Depending upon the type of appeal that you are filing (more on that in a minute), you may have to hire another lawyer who specializes in appellate practice, or, at the very least, you will have to give your attorney a separate retainer for the specific issue(s) being appealed. The amount of time it takes for an appeal to be decided varies, but generally an appeal can extend the time your divorce case takes to complete by *at least* one year. During the time it takes for the appeal to go through, your divorce case itself will be in limbo.

The rest of this answer discusses the detailed requirements for filing an appeal in New Jersey. The types of appeals and technicalities involved are reviewed, as are practical tips to keep in mind when considering an appeal.

Two types of appeals are allowed in New Jersey, interlocutory and of final orders. An appeal of a final order, in the divorce context, means that you are appealing the Judgment of Divorce. An appeal of any other order issued by the judge during your divorce case is called an interlocutory appeal. In the divorce context, most appeals are interlocutory in nature.

In general, when considering an interlocutory appeal, your attorney will have to file a motion for "leave to appeal." This means that your attorney will ask the Appellate Division for permission to appeal the order "in the interest of justice," because it is not the final Judgment of Divorce. The Appellate Division may or may not grant your motion. Interlocutory orders regarding custody are usually allowed to be brought to the Appellate Division.

Assuming the Appellate Division does grant your motion, the next step is to file a Notice of Appeal, filing fee and a Civil Appeal Case Information Statement. As the party filing the appeal, you are called the "appellant." Your attorney will have to order the transcript from the hearing and ensure that the correct number of copies are supplied to the Appellate Division and your soon-to-be former spouse, now called the "appellee." Thereafter, an appellate brief together with appendices must be filed by your lawyer; the appellee then files an opposition with appendices; and finally, your attorney can file a reply brief. If requested, the Appellate Division can grant oral argument in which both attorneys have a maximum of 30 minutes to argue their sides before the three-judge panel in the Appellate Division. The Appellate Division will issue its ruling on your appeal at a later date, usually six months to a year after oral argument is heard.

With an appeal of a final Judgment of Divorce, your attorney will have to follow all of the steps just outlined, with the exception of filing a motion for leave to appeal. All final orders are appealable as of right, which means that you don't have to ask permission to file your appeal. Your lawyer will just start the process by filing a Notice of Appeal. Please note that a Marital Settlement Agreement is an agreement between you and your former spouse and is *not* considered a final order for the purposes of an appeal. The Judgment of Divorce that is appealable is one that is issued by the judge after a trial, not simply one that approves your Marital Settlement Agreement. If you have second thoughts about some of the clauses in your Marital Settlement Agreement, in nearly every case you would not appeal to the Appellate Division but rather your experienced divorce attorney will recommend that you return to the judge and seek to either modify the agreement or reopen your divorce case for that purpose.

It is important to keep in mind that less than 25 percent of all appeals in the divorce context are won by the person bringing the appeal. The reason for this low success rate is the standard of review applied by the Appellate Division to the family court judge's ruling. The Appellate Division does not allow you to retry your divorce proceeding. Rather, the three-judge panel will not disturb any findings of fact made by your family court judge, but only looks to see if any mistakes or misapplications of law were made, and whether credible evidence supported the judge's ruling.

Now, after having your appeal heard by the Appellate Division, you still may not be satisfied that justice was done. Your next, and essentially last, recourse is to appeal your case again, this time to the New Jersey Supreme Court. The New Jersey Supreme Court requires that you file permission to have your case heard before its nine-judge panel by way of a "Petition for Certification." This court only accepts cases that have novel issues, what's called a case of "first impression." As you might guess, having the New Jersey Supreme Court accept your petition is very rare. Your experienced divorce attorney will offer you guidance and advice through the procedures for the highest court in New Jersey.

If you are disheartened after reading this answer, don't be. We provide this information in the interests of full disclosure, so you know what you may be up against in the appeal arena. One other option to filing an appeal does exist, called the Civil Appeals Settlement Program. In this program, your appeal is taken before a retired judge whose goal is to help the parties reach a settlement. You must rely upon your experienced divorce attorney to identify issues that may be appealable, and to guide you through the appeals process. Be prepared for both the time and the expense associated with an appeal, but if you feel an order was improperly decided, this avenue certainly is available for you to attempt to correct the wrong.

CHAPTER THREE

14 Important Dos and Don'ts for a Successful New Jersey Divorce

Throughout the book, reference is made to achieving a "successful divorce." Most people think that term is an oxymoron, like "jumbo shrimp" or "recorded live." So, what is meant by a "successful divorce"? Well, it's where both parties act like grownups in making decisions that will impact their future. It means not being overly willful or spiteful, and fighting over assets just for the sake of punishing the other person. It means putting your children's needs ahead of your own. It means ending your marriage with your head held high, and moving on to a happier, more fulfilling life.

A divorce requires you to understand that you are undoing a financial, emotional and physical partnership. A successful divorce is not some pie-in-the-sky fantasy but rather a very achievable goal. At this point, you may not believe it's possible, but the following 14 important dos and don'ts will set you on the right path. After all, you deserve success and a brand-new, happy life!

DOS

1. *Consider Hiring a Therapist and/or Marriage Counselor*

Before you decide that divorce is the right path for you, you should seriously consider seeing a therapist, preferably two: a marriage counselor for you and your spouse, and one just for you. As you have learned in this book, the legal process of getting divorced involves time and money, and you need to be certain that your marriage cannot be fixed before embarking upon this journey. Assuming your spouse agrees to attend marriage counseling with you, this might be an appropriate first step. A marriage saved certainly is a successful outcome.

If you have already tried marriage counseling, or you or your spouse do not want to participate in couple's therapy, then it's time to think about getting a therapist just for you. This is someone who will help you process all of your feelings and sort through the variety of emotions that you are, and will be, feeling over the course of your divorce. Your therapist will help you with the grieving process over the end of your marriage, and will help you to emerge stronger on the other side.

Moreover, a therapist may be a good person to have in your life even if you are already certain that you want a divorce. He or she could be an integral part of your support network in addition to your attorney, religious or spiritual leader, family and friends. A therapist is trained in helping people through an emotional crisis. He or she will offer you tools to assist you in moving forward. A therapist will listen to your situation and expertly help you cope and, eventually, flourish. Your health insurance may cover the costs associated with going to therapy, as therapy is recognized as contributing to a healthy life just as you would see a dentist or eye doctor. Think about whether a therapist and/ or marriage counselor is right for you.

2. *Take Care of You*

As a corollary to Step 1, another concrete step you can take toward a successful divorce is to take care of yourself. You must figure out who you are separate and apart from your spouse. For some people this is an exciting exercise, while for others, it can be quite daunting. But it is a necessary step for everyone involved in a divorce.

How do you embark upon creating a separate identity? Uncover your interests. What captivates your imagination? If you enjoy cooking, take a cooking class. If you like reading, join a book club. Have you always dreamed of getting into the cage at the Ultimate Fighting Championship? Take a Brazilian Jiu-Jitsu class. No judgments, no criticisms; take time to explore your needs and desires.

You also must look after your own health. Do you need to lose some weight? Tone up your muscles? Improve your diet? Get a checkup? This is one aspect of your life that you can take control of during a time when you may feel everything is spiraling out of control. "Taking care of you" means that you put yourself first, perhaps for the first time in a long while. Join a gym, see a nutritionist, go to your doctor, take a hike, lift weights, run, bike ride or swim. Make sure that you are physically in a good place. When you are healthy, you will sleep better and have a more positive attitude. You also will have more energy, which will be invaluable as you undergo the divorce process.

In addition to getting support from your friends, you will also make new friends as you expand your interests. All of this is healthy. Do not feel like you are being a burden on your family and friends, as they truly do want to support you now. Give yourself permission to "take care of you" and you may soon be happily surprised with the person looking back at you in the mirror.

Often, people dive into work when they are going through a divorce. While working can help you take your mind off your situation, it could also be an avoidance mechanism. Obviously, you need to work in order to make money and pay your bills. When you are divorcing, however, it may not be the time to take on extra projects or a lot of overtime. Your work product may not be up to your usual standards as you will find yourself being distracted by many life-changing decisions as you navigate through your divorce. It is advisable to do the best job you can in your workplace, but also to take the time to "take care of you."

Another potential avoidance mechanism may come from a surprising source: your children. Chauffeuring your kids to their many activities, going to every single one of their games, helping them with their homework, and so forth, is more than a full-time job. It is very easy to get caught up in your children's lives and, thereby, evade dealing with your own. By putting yourself first and working on your own issues, you actually will become a better parent. You will find appropriate outlets for the anger, hurt, resentment and jealousy, and spend better quality time together with your children. Let a friend or relative help out with the chauffeuring and other child-related duties, if possible, while you try to spend some time on you. You will be happier and more relaxed. And, believe it or not, your kids will notice the difference.

"Taking care of you" is not selfish. It is exploring aspects of your personality or life that have been dormant for years, or even nonexistent. If your divorce includes joint physical custody of the children, or multiple day visitation periods, you may find yourself alone in your house for the first time in years or even decades. It isn't healthy to sit around watching television, just waiting for your kids to return. In order to have a successful divorce, your life has to change in positive new ways. Isn't it time to meet the new you?

3. *Start saving money!*

Whether you are a "breadwinning" or "nonbreadwinning" spouse, it is important that you start saving money now so that you can better support yourself financially during the pendency of the divorce and once your divorce is final. If you were the sole "breadwinning" spouse in your marriage, the court will likely order you to pay spousal support and/or child support. This means that, in addition to your own living expenses, you are going to have to contribute substantially to the living expenses of your soon-to-be ex-spouse and children. Providing money for two households can be very difficult financially and could cause you to have to change your lifestyle significantly, especially if you have not saved any money in anticipation of divorce.

If you were a "nonbreadwinning" spouse in the marriage, you should not put yourself in a situation where you and your children are living support check-to-support check, with no money available until the support money comes in. What if the check is late, or doesn't come at all? You will have to go back to court and seek enforcement of the spousal support or child support order, but that will take time. You want to be able to take care of yourself financially in the meantime, and that's why you should start saving your money as soon as thoughts of divorce enter the picture.

4. *Copy All Financial Records Now*

One of the first things we ask our clients to provide to us are copies of important financial documents that reflect family finances, personal assets, your soon-to-be ex-spouse's income and assets, and so forth. So start copying now! And do this before you tell your spouse anything about wanting a divorce. (Sometimes important documents have a way of "getting lost" once your spouse knows you will be filing for divorce).

The information contained in these documents will form the basis of your Case Information Statement and will be used in determining support payments, among other things.

You may be wondering what constitutes "financial documents." Or, exactly what documentation you should be gathering. Well, the following list is very long, but try to copy as many of these documents as you have access to at the beginning of the divorce process so that you don't have to worry about finding them months down the road. Just tell your lawyer which documents don't apply in your situation, as well as which ones do apply but you cannot locate. Then, go back and look for the missing documents. Getting this task checked off early in the process will enable you to move forward and plan for your future rather than having to keep looking through old files from your past.

Here is an *exhaustive* list of financial documents that your lawyer will want to review, if you have them. Please keep in mind that not all of these documents may apply to your particular circumstance. If you don't know what the document is, chances are it is not applicable to your situation. Also, do not put off meeting with an attorney because you cannot find some of these documents.

(1) *Filed Income Tax Returns.* Complete personal income tax returns for the past three to five years, such as Form 1040 or Form 1040 EZ and corresponding New Jersey (and/or another state) returns. If you cannot locate these, you will want to check with your tax preparer for copies.

(2) *Proof of Current Income.* Documents showing both of your and your ex-spouse's incomes for this year (and for last year, if your tax returns haven't been filed yet), such as W-2 forms, 1099 forms and interest and dividend income [from your bank(s) or brokerage account(s)], as well as paycheck stubs covering the most recent three months. Remember to include any lottery winnings as well as both of your most recent Social Security statements.

(3) *Real Estate.* As to all real property owned by you and/or your spouse, provide copies of the deed conveying title, promissory note, mortgage or deed of trust, payment coupon or invoice for your most recent mortgage payment, a statement from the lender of the balance due on the mortgage, any appraisals conducted with regard to the property and the most recent property tax bill. On a related note, provide copies of any second mortgages or lines of credit issued on the property, including the payment coupon or invoice for your most recent payment and a statement from the lender of the balance due on such secondary lien. Additionally, copies of the property insurance policies including the carrier's name, policy number, coverage and term. Real property includes your marital residence, second or vacation home(s), timeshares and any rental property (with a statement of rental income).

(4) *Motor Vehicles.* As to all cars, trucks, motorcycles, and the like, owned by you and/or your spouse, provide copies of the title and registration, promissory note (if the vehicle is not owned outright), the payment coupon or invoice for your most recent payment and a statement by you as to the mileage and condition of the vehicle. Additionally, copies of the vehicle's insurance policies including the carrier's name, policy number, coverage and term.

(5) *Life Insurance.* As to any life insurance policies owned by you and/or your spouse, provide a copy of the policy, or a copy of the policy summary that shows the name and address of the insurance company, policy number, the owner of the policy and beneficiary(ies),

amount of the death benefit, cash value (if any) and amount of the premium.

(6) *Health Insurance.* As to any health insurance policies available to you, provide a copy of the plan summary that shows the name and address of the health insurance company, policy number, group number and/or ID number, beneficiaries of the policy and a summary of the benefits, including copay and deductible amounts. Don't forget any long-term care and disability insurance policies that are separate from coverage and automatically included with your salary as a benefit.

(7) *Bank, Brokerage and Retirement Accounts.* As to any financial/brokerage/retirement accounts such as checking, savings, certificates of deposit, IRA, 401(k), 403(b), annuities, SERP, SEP, Keogh, UGMA/UTMA, 529 plans, pension or publicly or privately traded securities or stock accounts, provide documents that show the name and address of the institution, account number, owner of the account, identity of any person authorized to sign checks or access the accounts, current balance of the account, copies of quarterly statements for the past one to three years and monthly statements for the past one to three years. In addition, copies of the signature cards for your safety deposit box and a list of its contents.

(8) *Business Owned.* As to any business in which you have an ownership interest, provide copies of the Articles of Incorporation and By-laws, partnership agreement, corporate records and books (if available), stock certificates (including any restrictions on transfer),

buy/sell agreements, year-end financial statements for prior calendar or fiscal year, the most recent balance sheet and/or profit and loss statement and the most recent tax returns. For any real property owned by the business, provide the information listed in the Real Estate section and show the percentage of ownership attributed to you.

(9) *Personal Property.* A list of your valuables such as art, jewelry, furniture, paintings, antiques and collectibles and their corresponding current market value, purchase price, source of funds used for the purchase and outstanding payments. In addition, any inheritance and interest in a trust. Make sure you identify all such property owned separately by you or your spouse at the time you were married.

(10) *Legal Documents.* While not specifically financial in nature, copies of the following legal documents will be of interest to your divorce attorney: will, living will, power of attorney, healthcare proxy, prenuptial or postnuptial agreement, and Divorce Decree and Order of Child/Spousal Support from a previous marriage or relationship.

(11) *Credit Cards and Other Debt.* For credit cards (whether joint or individual), provide one to three years of statements. As to any other debt (such as student loans, medical bills, prior child support/alimony obligations, and/or tax liens/debts owed the IRS), provide copies of the promissory notes and most recent payment coupon or invoice. Additionally, provide copies of your utility bills (electric, gas, telephone, oil, television, Internet, and so forth) for the past one to three months.

This list is *not* meant to scare you, but rather to perhaps jog your memory about an asset you may have overlooked. Your experienced divorce attorney will discuss with you the specific documents needed for your case. Putting off the task of gathering documents, unfortunately, will not make this obligation disappear. So, roll up your sleeves and look through your files. Once you've finished this task, you'll be well on your way to putting the past behind you and starting with your new, successful life.

5. *Establish Your Own Credit, if You Have Not Done So while in the Marriage*

One of the initial steps you can take toward a new life is to get your financial house in order. You may have joint bank accounts and joint credit cards with your soon-to-be former spouse, and, if you are a nonworking spouse, you may not have any credit in your own name. Now is the time to start to change all that!

First things first: Request your credit report. You don't have to contact one of those companies that advertise with pirates, waiters and catchy jingles and pay for a copy of your report, either. Under federal law, you are able to get a copy of your credit report, *for free*, every 12 months by contacting one (or all three) of the credit reporting agencies: Experian (www.experian. com), TransUnion (www.transunion.com) and Equifax (www. experian.com). Because you live in New Jersey, requesting your free credit reports is easy; all you have to do is contact the credit reporting agencies directly. Most other states do not have this perk!

A credit report is simply a document that itemizes all of your accounts, balances and payment history. Please note that a credit report does *not* give your credit score (FICO), which is the three-digit gauge of your creditworthiness. When you receive your free credit report, review it very carefully. Contact the credit bureau from which you received the report and notify it of any inaccuracies. Then, follow up to ensure the proper changes are made.

Once you are satisfied that your credit report is 100 percent accurate, the next item on your agenda is to establish credit in your own name. Do not close or freeze any joint accounts without first speaking with your divorce attorney, however, as an agreement or Order of the Court needs to be in place before taking such action.

How do you go about building up your own credit history as a single person? While this may sound intimidating, it is more about baby steps and waiting than it is time-consuming or difficult. Get a job, at least part-time. This will require you to pay taxes to the IRS and allow you to pay your debts as they become due. It also will enable you to rent or purchase a home if you are going to be moving out of or selling the marital residence. For obvious reasons, landlords and lenders like to see steady employment before signing on the dotted line.

After you have opened up your own checking and savings accounts, apply for a credit card in your own name. Make sure to check for the lowest interest rate possible. If you have no or poor credit history, you may want to apply for a department store credit card instead of a Visa, MasterCard, Discover or American Express. In whatever form you obtain your own credit card, make sure to promptly pay your bills, in full. This will increase your credit score significantly.

If you are denied credit from these sources, look into applying for a secured credit card. This essentially is a prepaid debit card, where you put all of the money into an account and when you make purchases, the money is drawn down. Given today's economic clime, many banks and credit unions offer this option. Just make sure that your institution informs the credit reporting agencies of your account history in order to ensure your responsible behavior is reflected on your credit report.

Another potential source of credit is a car loan. Because this is secured by the vehicle itself, you may qualify for a car loan even if you don't have a traditional credit card. Once again, make sure to pay your car payments in full, on time, and you'll reap the credit score rewards sooner than you might think.

Remember, rebuilding or establishing your own credit is a marathon, not a sprint. Choose your credit applications wisely and don't go overboard. A couple of accounts with a flawless payment history will stand you in great stead for your future.

6. *Hire the Right Divorce Attorney for You*

When you choose a doctor, it is important that you find one who is knowledgeable in his or her particular specialty. You probably also care about his or her "bedside manner." Some people want a doctor who will tell them every ailment they could possibly have while others want a doctor who is a "nonalarmist" and only tells them what the doctor feels they really need to know.

It is not much different with attorneys. If you are seeking a divorce, you want an attorney who specializes in the practice of divorce, but you also want an attorney whose style, demeanor and attitude meshes well with yours. The good news is that, unlike in the medical profession where insurance companies restrict you to using doctors within a particular "network," it is far less restrictive to choose a divorce attorney. But, how do you choose?

In the next section of the book, we will provide you with some tips on hiring the right divorce attorney for you.

7. *Be Truthful with Your Divorce Attorney*

As has been repeated many times throughout this book, your divorce attorney is your trusted guide — your legal representative

— your advocate. In order for your lawyer to be as effective as possible, he or she must know the facts of your particular circumstances. All of the facts. Not just the ones you *prefer* to share. If you don't tell your divorce attorney certain truths, those truths may come out anyway — by your spouse's attorney! The last thing you want is for your attorney to be blindsided by damaging facts he or she knew nothing about.

Your divorce attorney sincerely wants to help you through this difficult process. However, he or she only has your word about the facts of your marriage and will build a strategy around that information. Rest assured that everything you discuss is protected by the attorney-client privilege (unless, of course, you confess to a crime about to be committed!). Your lawyer is not going to judge you for your decisions; he or she only wants to know all of the facts in order to protect you the best way possible. To receive the most effective representation possible, you cannot conceal facts you believe to be harmful to your case, nor fabricate information about your former spouse to your attorney. Failures to disclose truths or telling outright lies are usually discovered, which puts your lawyer in the bad position of having to change course midstream. And that can only hurt you.

People sometimes don't come clean with their divorce attorney for a variety of reasons. Usually, clients hide a piece of information that they feel could hurt the case. Other reasons for concealing the truth include being embarrassed, trying to improve their image, making themselves sound/feel better, avoiding perceived criticism, religious/ethical considerations, shifting blame, saving face and avoiding confrontation. Still others think a lie will give them a leg up in the litigation, or just want to tell their lawyer what they think he or she wants to hear. Others do not want to admit to having a drug or alcohol problem. It may have been hard to come to grips with why their marriage is ending, and confessing that truth to another person, even their lawyer, can make it a painful reality.

Whatever the motivation, hiding the truth or being dishonest is not going to advance your case. For example, if you have met someone new and you think that marriage may be on the horizon, tell your lawyer. Why? Should you be receiving spousal support, your lawyer will make sure to protect your interests in the Marital Settlement Agreement. If you tell your attorney that your former spouse went away on vacation and forfeited her visitation, when in fact you took the children to Disney World, your attorney won't be able to properly defend you should a motion, with photos, be filed. If you think something is not important, tell your divorce attorney anyway. It may become integral to your case! Your experienced divorce attorney must have all the facts, be they good, bad or ugly, so that he or she can represent you in the best way possible. Never lose sight of your ultimate goal of having a successful divorce, which means that any potentially damaging issues are revealed and discussed early on, and a strategy devised to address them. You don't want a hidden issue to surface at the worst possible time, and it always does. Share all of your information openly and honestly with your attorney, and you soon will be realizing a successful divorce in New Jersey.

DON'TS

1. Don't Move Out of Your House

Unless there is domestic violence taking place in your home, do not even think of moving out of your house before you speak to an attorney. If you leave your home, it could ultimately result in your having to pay more spousal support or could cause you to be unable to collect spousal support. Your experienced divorce attorney can explain to you the potential consequences of a decision to move out of your home. Be armed with knowledge before you take a foolish and impulsive step.

There are a number of reasons why this is so important. First, by moving out of your home and leaving the children behind, you are indicating to the court that you have no problems with your spouse having full physical custody of the children. While that might, in fact, be the case, it is a decision that you want to make after having had the opportunity to speak with your divorce attorney about your rights in your particular situation. It is not a decision you want to be forced upon you when that is not what you had intended.

Moreover, moving out of your house, in the absence of domestic violence, could send a signal to the court that you can easily afford to pay for your own residence and your spouse's residence. (That is, unless you moved to a residence that does not cost you anything, such as your parents' home or a friend's home).

If the fighting in your home has become unbearable (but not physically threatening), the two of you can remain in the house together if you set up some ground rules. If the house is large enough to divide into two separate "sections," that is probably the best way to go. We all remember the episode of *I Love Lucy* where Lucy and Ricky divided their apartment in half after they had a fight. The problem was, Lucy was able to leave the apartment because the front door was on her side and Ricky was able to take care of certain needs that Lucy couldn't because the bathroom was on Ricky's side. Obviously, *I Love Lucy* was a comedy and your divorce is real life. Only you know if your home is capable of being "divided" so that both you and your spouse can continue to live there together, but apart.

Some couples actually choose to divide their *time* in the house, not the house itself. That is, one spouse lives in the house (with the children) for two weeks or a month, then the other spouse lives in the house (with the children) for two weeks or a month. This arrangement can present a lot of logistical problems and doesn't work out very well most of the time, but it is an option you can discuss with your ex if you truly cannot stand to live in the house together until the divorce is final.

2. Don't Start a Business or Make a Major Purchase Before Filing for Divorce

In New Jersey, every asset acquired *from the date of marriage to the filing of the divorce complaint* is subject to equitable distribution. Therefore, if you are seriously thinking about divorce, now is not the time to purchase a new boat or start a new business. Even if assets are bought in your name, or you are the legal owner of the business, if the boat/business was purchased/started before filing for divorce, it becomes a marital asset to be divided between you and your spouse. Far better to wait until the divorce complaint is filed before making major purchases or starting a new business.

3. Don't Say Anything on the Telephone that You Would Not Want the Judge to Hear

While you are going through a divorce, always presume that your every telephone conversation with your spouse is being taped, and don't say anything that could damage your credibility or reputation before the court. New Jersey permits the taping of telephone conversations if one party consents; that is, if you are talking on the telephone with your spouse, and your spouse "consents" to the taping of the call (and obviously he or she consents if he/she is the one taping the call!), your consent is not required. The tape recording is perfectly legal and can probably be used as evidence against you in the divorce.

This brings to mind the recent custody proceedings between Hollywood actor Mel Gibson and the mother of his child,

Oksana Grigorieva. Gibson yelled profanities and furiously threatened Grigorieva while she was taping all of his telephone calls. Because he is a celebrity, it all ended up on the Internet and the incident was the repeated topic of late-night television monologues. More importantly, these telephone recordings likely will have some effect on his court proceedings when deciding custody issues concerning his infant daughter.

Now, you are probably not a celebrity and will likely not have to worry about your recordings being played on the *Tonight Show*. However, offensive or threatening recordings can be brought into court and not only can embarrass you but can also cause serious damage to you in your divorce/custody matter.

Always speak carefully when conversing with your soon-to-be ex-spouse. That is a good rule to live by in any case, as it will make the divorce proceedings less unpleasant overall, and hopefully, easier to resolve.

4. Don't Do Anything that Will Make You "Look Bad" to the Judge

A corollary to the last "Don't" is this: Don't do anything while a divorce is pending that would make you look bad before the judge. For example, if you are hoping to minimize the amount of spousal support you will have to pay, and your attorney is arguing that you are having trouble making ends meet (which is what you have told your attorney!), don't decide to take your new girlfriend on a luxury cruise around the world or on a fabulous vacation to Brazil. Your soon-to-be ex-spouse is sure to find out about it, and you can bet that it will be reported to the court by your spouse's attorney. And the judge will never believe another word you or your attorney say.

In addition, watch what you reveal about yourself on social networking sites like Facebook. You don't want to joke about all of your weekends out getting drunk when you are in the midst of a custody battle. Nor do you want to brag about a job promotion and a higher salary, or post photographs of the Maserati you plan on buying as soon as your divorce becomes final.

Finally, don't make frustrated and angry faces while in court for a hearing or a trial, or give dirty looks to your spouse. And don't ever get nasty and argumentative with the judge! Judges are only human and are bound to be affected by whether he/she thinks you are a "good" person or a "bad" person. And your behavior in and out of court can reveal a lot to the court.

5. Don't Have Sex with Your Ex

When you stop and think about it, this is really a no-brainer. Even though you are now divorcing, you once thought you were in love with this person. Sex can only wreak havoc with your emotions at this very stressful time. Unless you have decided you want to reconcile, and sense that your spouse feels the same way, having sex with the person you are now divorcing is likely a big mistake. It can lead to confusion and hurt feelings, and usually is a step backward on your path to a new life.

One of our clients decided it was a good idea to have sex with his ex. "How could it hurt?" he thought. Well, the next morning, his spouse thought the divorce was now "off," and had already told the children that "Mommy and Daddy are getting back together." That would have been great, if that is what they both wanted. But it wasn't what the client wanted. When he told his ex that he wanted to continue going forward with the divorce, his spouse told him she felt used, and his children were once again devastated by the fact that their parents were not getting back together. DON'T DO IT.

6. Never Speak Badly of Your Spouse in Front of Your Children

Obviously, a divorce is difficult on the husband and wife going through it. Untangling the partnership made during the marriage — emotionally and financially — is challenging under the best of circumstances. If children are involved, the process may become even more complex. One concrete step you can take toward a better future for you and you children is to make the conscious decision not to speak badly about your spouse in front of them. *Ever.*

Think about it. Children are the combination of you and your spouse. Naturally, they love both of you. The fact that you and your spouse are divorcing does not mean that either one of you loves your children less. And the converse is true: Children do not love either parent less because they are getting divorced. Therein lies the guilt.

It has been well documented that many children feel guilty over their parents' divorce. They feel as if they were its cause. One of your goals in having a successful divorce is to ensure that your children do not carry such needless guilt. So, how do you do this?

- Do not use your children as pawns during the legal divorce process.
- Do not use your children as spies to learn about your ex-spouse's current exploits.
- Do not use your children as messengers.
- Do not impede your children's visitation with your former spouse.
- Above all, do not speak badly about your ex-spouse in front of your children. And don't allow friends and family members to do so either.

As parents, you are the adults in the relationship with your children. In your divorce, your ultimate goal should be to become successful co-parents. This means that, if the court awards joint legal custody, you and your former spouse will together have to make all important decisions about your child's education, activities and health — all with the best interests of your child in mind, regardless of any personal animosity you may feel toward the other parent. Therefore, you will have to communicate with your former spouse directly.

Sometimes communicating with the spouse you are divorcing can be extremely difficult. If you have children, however, you do not have a choice. You may want to discuss your decisions with your ex-spouse via e-mail or text, if face-to-face or a telephone call are not good options. A word of caution: If you are talking on the telephone, make sure you are aware of your surroundings, as little ears may be lurking around the corner. If an in-person meeting cannot be avoided, schedule it for a public place, such as a Starbucks or local diner. Create a list of topics about the children and don't deviate from the list; rehashing what brought you to divorce is counterproductive. These discussions need to be held outside of the presence of your children, who should not become privy to their contents. If you find the need to vent, do so with your therapist or friends. You don't want to hurt your children any more by unloading on them, no matter their ages.

On a related note, make it a top priority not to put your children in the middle or take sides. Clearly, you never, *ever*, should ask your children which parent they like better or which parent they think is "right" in particular arguments. But, much more subtle ways of mentally manipulating your children should be avoided as much as possible. Choose your words carefully. Instead of saying, "If your mom ever paid me the child support she owes, I would be able to buy you that game," try "That game looks like it might be interesting. We have to wait a while, and hopefully we can get it for you soon." Similarly, a better alternative to calling your child when s/he is with your ex-spouse and saying "I miss you" might be "I hope you're having a good time with Dad. I love you." A hostile environment is not healthy for your child, who now more than ever needs to feel loved and safe.

Remember, when you criticize your former spouse, your child may think you are criticizing one-half of him/her as well.

You will not have to go through this process alone. In addition to your therapist, the court system has set up a program to help you transition into being a single parent. As discussed previously, you will be required to attend a Parent Education Class shortly after your case is filed, for a nominal fee. This class is led by a licensed therapist, and goes over, in depth, the issues covered in this section as well as many more. In addition, during the class you will receive instruction and tips on ways to open the lines of communication between you and your former spouse as it relates to your children. You also will learn strategies to protect your children, as much as possible, from being inappropriately used during the divorce process and beyond. In the end, your divorce will be successful only when you and your children thrive in your new life.

7. Don't Be Afraid to Ask Your Divorce Attorney Questions

You probably have heard the saying, "There are no dumb questions." Never is this more true than in the legal arena. Unless you are a lawyer yourself, specializing in family law, it is totally expected that you will not know all of the intricacies involved with seeking a divorce.

Your experienced divorce attorney wants to guide you through the legal process and make it as smooth and painless as is possible. With the goal of making you comfortable during the pendency of your case, your lawyer will explain to you legal details, strategies and options. He or she will need to know all of the facts of your married life in order to put your best case forward. Necessarily, he or she will be asking you many, many questions.

But, this is not a one-way street. If your lawyer poses a question or explains a legal procedure that you do not fully understand, simply *ask*. This is your life, your divorce, and you deserve full disclosure and comprehension. Every person brings to the table a different set of education and life experiences. It is part of your attorney's job to ensure that you are completely comfortable every step of the way.

Here's a suggestion: Prior to every meeting with your attorney, write down a list of questions that you need answered related to the topics that you will cover. That way, you'll think through issues and be prepared with your questions before the meeting begins. Try to brainstorm and figure out what you will want to know related to your divorce process. To help with this, you may want to speak with your therapist or trusted friend or family member to explore the issues. Your attorney wants you to be comfortable with the decisions and strategies and thoroughly understand why each was made.

On a related note, be very careful what you discuss with your friends, and do not bring a friend with you to your meetings with your divorce attorney. This is because your lawyer needs to protect the "attorney-client privilege." What is the "attorney-client privilege," you ask? Good question! This "privilege" or legal doctrine means that any communications between you and your lawyer are confidential and can never be disclosed to your spouse's attorney in the discovery process. The "privilege" is broken if your attorney gives you legal advice in front of another person, or if you tell your friends exactly what you and your attorney talked about. Then, all bets are off and your spouse's attorney can learn everything that was said in front of or to that person, and your legal strategies could be in jeopardy. If this explanation isn't clear to you, make sure you discuss it with your attorney until you perfectly understand this very important concept.

When it comes to having a firm grasp on your legal positions, it is imperative that all of your questions are answered to your complete satisfaction. Do not hesitate to explore the whys and wherefores with your experienced divorce attorney. This is your divorce; your lawyer is only your guide. For you to have a successful divorce, you need to be at ease with the decisions made along the way. One way to do this is to truly understand your options and select the right course for you. Remember, the only dumb question is the one not asked.

CHAPTER FOUR

Tips on Hiring the Right Divorce Attorney for You

As discussed earlier in our section on divorce "myths," two of the most important things to keep in mind when choosing a divorce attorney are the following: (1) he or she must be extremely knowledgeable and experienced in the area of divorce/family law; and (2) he or she must "fit" well with you.

The first qualification is easy to ascertain — just ask the attorney about his or her experience in this area of the law. The second qualification — fit — is more difficult to determine. You alone know what you want and need from your divorce attorney. One size does not fit all.

Is it important to you that your attorney be emotionally supportive as well as legally proficient? Then you must make sure, during the initial consultation, that the attorney is ready, willing and able to provide some "handholding" to you, in addition to his/her legal expertise. Divorce is not "business as usual" — it may be the most emotional time of your life — and if you feel you need an attorney who is sensitive to your emotions, you must make sure that you choose an attorney who will be.

Moreover, you want to hire an attorney who will agree with your "philosophy" of the case. Do you want an attorney who will try to keep things calm and low-key and complete the divorce in the quickest and least-painful manner possible? If so, make sure your attorney is ready to act according to your wishes. On the other hand, do you want an attorney who is very aggressive and will fight for everything he or she can get from your spouse? If you feel you want to fight for every little thing, don't care how much money you spend, nor how much animosity is created between you and your spouse as a result, then your divorce attorney must be "on board" for that type of contentious divorce as well. This is something you need to discuss in your initial consultation.

By far the most common complaint made against divorce attorneys is that they do not return their clients' telephone calls in a punctual manner. When asked about this, attorneys who don't promptly return calls will usually say that they "didn't call the client back because nothing new has happened in his case." That is not an acceptable answer. An attorney should return the client's call promptly and simply inform the client that nothing new has happened in his/her case. Sometimes that is all a client wants to hear —an update to learn that there is no update.

The bottom line is, if you call your divorce attorney, your call should always be returned within 24 hours or less (absent emergency). At your initial consultation with an attorney, you should ask what the attorney's policy is on returned calls. If the attorney tells you that he/she will return calls within two or three days, you may want to think about crossing that attorney off your list. In addition, your divorce attorney should be willing to give you his/her cell phone number so you can reach him/her if something serious occurs that could impact your case.

As we've been saying throughout this book, divorce is a very emotional time. While you should not be calling your attorney every hour on the hour, a good divorce attorney must recognize that you may be in a fragile state and need some "handholding" in addition to expert legal guidance. A great divorce attorney should recognize this and be emotionally supportive of his/her clients.

The following are some good questions to ask a prospective divorce attorney during an initial consultation (Feel free to ask us these questions if you meet with us for an initial consultation!):

- How many years have you been practicing divorce/family law?
- How many years have you been practicing divorce/family law in New Jersey?
- What percentage of your cases are divorce/family law cases?
- Have you handled divorces like mine before?
- Do you have experts (forensic accountants, bankruptcy attorneys, psychologists, and so forth) you regularly work with, if needed?
- Will you be the person responsible for strategizing about and negotiating my divorce?
- Will you take my input into consideration while planning strategy?
- Do you encourage or discourage clients from negotiating directly with their spouses?
- What is your policy about returning clients' calls?
- Are you willing to give me your cell phone number in case I really need to reach you? (An attorney who says "no" may not be the right attorney for you).
- Will I receive copies of all legal documents?
- What are your fees per hour?
- How much money do I need to give you for a retainer?
- What are the hourly rates for the other professionals in your office (associates, paralegals, and others) who may work on my divorce?
- Do you charge for faxes, copies and long-distance telephone calls at cost? If not, what is your markup?
- What's your estimate of the total cost for this divorce?
- Do you think I will get everything I am asking for in this divorce?

The last two questions are tricky ones but are very good questions to ask. In truth, no one will be able to answer them definitively, as so much depends on the individual circumstances of your case and how everything unfolds. But these are good questions to ask during an initial consultation because how they are answered will reveal a lot about an attorney. An honest attorney will tell you that these questions are too difficult to answer with certainty — but he or she can give you a general range of fees and a sense of how likely you are to get what you are asking for. A dishonest attorney may quote you a very low rate, or promise you everything you are asking for, just to get your business. But, you want an attorney who is honest with you from the outset! These questions will help you figure that out during your first meeting.

NEXT STEPS

We hope that you have found this book helpful as you begin taking those next steps on your journey to your new life. Remember that this book cannot provide you with specific legal advice, nor can it substitute for the guidance of an experienced divorce attorney.

If you have decided that you want to file for divorce, or you have been served with divorce papers by your spouse, and you reside in Northern or Central New Jersey, we welcome you to contact us for a complimentary one-hour consultation so we can determine if we are a good fit to work together. If you ultimately decide not to hire us, or if we decline your case, we will provide you with a list of other experienced divorce attorneys in your area to help you continue your search for the right divorce attorney for you.

Our New Jersey office is located in Fairfield (Essex County). Our complimentary initial consultations are offered at this office. If Fairfield is not convenient for you, we have "satellite" offices in several other areas of New Jersey and can arrange to meet you at one of these offices. Call our office for more information at 973-233-4080.

If you reside in Southern New Jersey, feel free to call us for a referral to a divorce attorney in your area.

Remember: Divorce does not have to be devastating. In fact, it actually can be liberating — freeing you to pursue interests you've been ignoring and to create a whole new life for yourself! We hope the information we have provided in this book has helped to set you on the right path to a successful New Jersey divorce!

To contact The Salvo Law Firm, P.C.

Call (973) 233-4080

Also, please visit our website at www.SalvoLawFirm.com.

9 781593 307028